SOMEWHERE IN FRANCE, SOMEWHERE IN GERMANY

A Combat Soldier's Journey through the Second World War

Francis P. Sempa

Hamilton Books
A member of
The Rowman & Littlefield Publishing Group
Lanham · Boulder · New York · Toronto · Plymouth, UK

Copyright © 2011 by
Hamilton Books
4501 Forbes Boulevard
Suite 200
Lanham, Maryland 20706
Hamilton Books Acquisitions Department (301) 459-3366

Estover Road
Plymouth PL6 7PY
United Kingdom

Library of Congress Control Number: 2011929918
ISBN: 978-0-7618-5608-5 (paperback : alk. paper)
eISBN: 978-0-7618-5609-2

Contents

Acknowledgments

My father was an infantry soldier with the 29th Division during the Second World War. He did not maintain a diary or a journal of his war experiences, but he did, as a dutiful son, write numerous letters to his parents (my grandparents) from stateside training camps, England, France, and Germany. A few years after my father's death (he died in 1988), my sister discovered these letters in a shoebox in the cellar of her home in Avoca, Pennsylvania. That was the house that my father lived in until he was drafted in April 1941 to serve in the United States Army.

This book would not have been possible without those letters. My father, like many of the soldiers who fought overseas during the Second World War, did not talk much about his wartime experiences. The letters, even with the limitations imposed by wartime censorship, provide an insight into the perceptions of a young man who was transformed from a civilian newspaper correspondent into a combat soldier in the most destructive war in human history. My father's original letters are housed at the U.S. Army War College in Carlisle, Pennsylvania, which takes pride in telling the story of the American Army "one soldier at a time."

The letters, however, are only given historical meaning by context, and that context is provided by the historians of the war, especially those who have written extensively about the 29th Division during World War II. First among those historians is Joseph Ewing who served in my father's regiment (the 175th) during the war and wrote the indispensable combat history of the division entitled *29 Let's Go*, published by the Infantry Journal Press in 1948.

Building on Ewing's work, historian Joseph Balkoski has written three excellent volumes on the 29th Division's combat in France: *Omaha Beach, Beyond the Beachhead*, and *From Beachhead to Brittany*.

David Garth and Charles H. Taylor in 1946 wrote the War Department's history of the Battle of St. Lo; a battle in which the 29th Division played a significant role which is detailed in their volume, entitled *St. Lo.*

Michael Reynolds in 2003 wrote *Eagles and Bulldogs*, which recounts the 29th Division's actions from Omaha Beach to St. Lo.

Jonathan Gawne's *1944, Americans in Brittany*, written in 2002, provided useful information about the Brest campaign.

Leo Daugherty's *Battle of the Hedgerows* and John McManus' *The Americans at Normandy* were also extremely useful as sources.

The 29th Division's After Action Reports, which can be accessed on the Maryland Military Historical Society website, are an indispensable resource for the combat activities of all the division's infantry regiments and support units. They are the foundation of any history of the division, its units, or its soldiers.

Broader historical works that proved very helpful are cited throughout the book and noted in the bibliography. Among these, perhaps the most useful was Russell Weigley's *Eisenhower's Lieutenants*, a two-volume work that covers in great detail the war in northwest Europe.

The *Scranton Times-Tribune* was very gracious in granting permission to quote from newspaper articles and to use a wartime photograph of my father on the cover of this book. Special thanks to the publishers and to Associate Editor Patrick McKenna.

Last, but not least, this book is dedicated to my brother, Msgr. John Sempa, and my two sisters, Barbe Sempa and Cheryl Radkiewicz, who helped me with memories of our father and who are his greatest legacy.

Preface

On June 6, 1994, the 50th anniversary of the D-Day invasion of Normandy, I wrote a brief guest column for the *Scranton Times* based on letters that my father wrote to his parents from France and Germany during the Second World War. Several years later, I wrote two more articles on my father's wartime service; one for *American Diplomacy*, a web-based journal that I help edit, and the other for the *Washington Times* newspaper, which at that time published a weekly military history page.

In 2009, University Press of America published my book, *America's Global Role: Essays and Reviews on National Security, Geopolitics, and War*, a collection of articles and book reviews that I had written for several publications between 1986 and 2009. One of the essays in that book was the article I wrote about my father's wartime service for *American Diplomacy*, and a friend of mine who read the book suggested to me that I should write a book about my father's service in World War II.

My father wrote hundreds of letters to his parents between April 1941 and July 1945. I read and re-read all of the letters--written from barracks at Ft. Meade in Maryland, tents at A.P. Hill Military Reservation in Virginia, training grounds in the Carolinas, Camp Blanding in Florida, training barracks in Scotland and England, and foxholes and cellars in France and Germany. Wartime censorship limited the content of the letters, but each letter was dated with a return address.

The stateside letters were from Ft. Meade or the other training installations. The letters from England, due to wartime secrecy, had a return address of New York City. The letters after D-Day were from "Somewhere in France," "Somewhere in Europe," or "Somewhere in Germany."

To make historical sense of the letters, it was necessary to become steeped in the history of my father's infantry division, the 29th. Fortunately, the 29th Division's After Action Reports are accessible to scholars and the public on the Maryland Military Historical Society's website, and fine historians such as Joseph Ewing and Joseph Balkoski have done much of the scholarly legwork. These and other sources enabled me to identify where my father's regiment, and in some cases his battalion, was throughout the war. Thus, when my father in his letters writes that he has been "busy," or the "going is rugged," the dates of the letters combined with the After Action Reports and other sources reveal that his regiment or battalion is fighting in the treacherous hedgerow country of France, or attacking toward the strategic town of St. Lo, or laying siege to the port of Brest, or breaching the Siegfried Line of Germany. This allows us to pierce the wartime censorship which imposed limitations on what combat soldiers could tell the folks back home.

As I wrote this book, I kept reflecting on the many times that I watched movies or documentaries about the Second World War with my father, but did not ask detailed questions about what he did, where he was, and what he saw during the war. I wish I had been more inquisitive, but I am not certain that my father would have been very receptive to my questions. War is a very terrible experience. Union General William T. Sherman defined war very simply as "cruelty." The savagery of war is not something fathers usually talk about in detail with their children.

Most sons look up to their fathers as role models. Even before I wrote this book, I looked upon my father that way. Researching and writing this book has made me appreciate him even more. The letters he wrote home to his parents and his wartime service reveal a courageous, brave, and caring young man. Remarkably, while he was fighting among hedgerows, participating in the capture of St. Lo, laying siege to Brest, and penetrating the Siegfried Line, his first concern was not himself, but the well-being of his mother and father. Just as later in life, his first concern was never himself, but always his children.

Introduction

Tom Brokaw called them "the greatest generation." They lived through the tough economic times of the Great Depression and fought in the most destructive war in human history. They returned home from the war (if they were fortunate) and worked on assembly lines, started small businesses, went to college and graduate schools, became doctors and lawyers, married, bought homes, reared children, retired, lived on to old age, and died.

The American soldiers who fought in the Second World War never thought of themselves as special, but they were. Their characters were shaped in part by hardship and war. Collectively, they rescued tens of millions of their fellow human beings from tyranny and oppression. They are history's greatest liberators. My father, Frank F. Sempa, was one of them.

The Second World War was the most momentous event in human history. Its origins and causes are the subject of numerous historical works. The great and prolific British historian Paul Johnson, in his masterful history of the Twentieth Century, *Modern Times*, noted that in the 1930s and early 1940s, the "Devils" nearly took over the world. Hitler, Stalin, and the Japanese militarists intended to expand the geographic reach of their totalitarian systems as far as possible. Their was no limit to their geopolitical ambitions or their willingness to enslave and kill in furtherance of those ambitions.

The United States entered the war reluctantly. Geography kept the war from our shores for a time. Geography also shaped how we fought the war. In the Pacific, island fighting meant that the Navy and Marines would play major roles (though the army under MacArthur played a key role in the southwest Pacific and the air corps contributed greatly with strategic bombing of Japan). The fighting in North Africa and the continent of Europe would be done by the army and the army air corps. Of course, the navy would be needed to get the troops there, and the offshore island of England would serve as the principal base of the liberation armies.

My father's journey through the Second World War began at Fort Meade, Maryland, continued at A.P. Hill Military Reservation in Virginia, the fields of the Carolinas, Camp Blanding in Florida, and Camp Kilmer, New Jersey. He crossed the Atlantic on the *Queen Elizabeth*, landed in Scotland, and moved to southern and coastal England.

On June 6, 1944, he was aboard a ship in the English Channel. The next day, D-Day plus 1, he landed on Omaha Beach in Normandy. He fought from hedgerow to hedgerow to get to St Lo. He traveled by jeep and truck to the Brittany Peninsula to capture the port of Brest. He traveled by train to Holland and Belgium, then crossed into Germany in late September-early October 1944.

From November 1944 through February-May 1945, he penetrated the fortifications of the Siegfried Line, crossed the Roer and Rhine Rivers, and ended up at the west bank of the Elbe River when Germany surrendered. This book is the story of my father's journey. It was a journey shared by hundreds of thousands of other Americans. It was, as my father later wrote, "the greatest battle of our lives."

CHAPTER 1

Letters in a Shoebox

On July 9, 1945, my father, Frank F. Sempa, boarded a bus at Fort Indiantown Gap, Pennsylvania, and journeyed home to Avoca, a small town in northeastern Pennsylvania. He had left Avoca more than four years earlier after being drafted into the United States Army in April 1941. He left his job as a correspondent for the *Scranton Tribune* and joined the 29th Division's 175th infantry regiment, which trained stateside at Fort Meade in Maryland, A.P. Hill Military Reservation in Virginia, the Carolinas, and Camp Blanding in Florida. In September 1942, the 29th Division moved to Camp Kilmer, New Jersey, for embarkation to England where it trained to take part in the Allied invasion of Nazi-occupied Europe.

My father's wartime journey took him to Omaha Beach on June 7, 1944 (D-Day plus one). From there, he and his regiment fought their way through the hedgerows of the Normandy countryside to St Lo. As other elements of the U.S. army moved east toward Paris and Germany's Siegfried Line, the 29th Division moved west from St Lo toward the Brittany Peninsula with orders to seize the French port of Brest, then serving as a submarine base for Hitler's navy. After three weeks of tough fighting at Brest, the Germans surrendered the city on September 18, 1944.

Following the Brest campaign, my father's unit was transported by train to Holland and Belgium near the German border. In early October 1944, the 29th Division crossed into Germany, seized several small towns, and set out to capture Julich. The attack and capture of Julich, however, was delayed due to the necessity of countering Germany's surprise attack through the Ardennes Forest, known to history as the Battle of the Bulge.

My father's regiment crossed the Roer River and entered Julich in January 1945, and within a month the 29th Division seized and occupied Munchen-Gladbach, the largest city in Germany captured by the U.S. Army up to that point in the war. U.S., British and allied armies advanced on a broad front against the German Reich, while the Soviet Army swept westward toward Berlin.

By V-E Day, May 8, 1945, my father's unit had reached the Elbe River where an entire German V-2 rocket division surrendered to the 29th Division. A few days before, my father's division liberated a German slave labor camp near Dinslaken.

Troops were sent home according to a point system which took into consideration days spent in combat, the number of campaigns, and other factors. A soldier needed 84 points to go home; my father had 110. He declined the offer of a battlefield commission—three years of training and 11 months of combat, he thought, was enough.

His wartime service to his country was reflected on his uniform: the Arrowhead for participating in the Normandy invasion; four campaign ribbons; the Good Conduct Medal; the prestigious Combat Infantryman's Badge; and the Bronze Star. By war's end, he had reached the rank of Master Sergeant.

He returned to his job at the *Scranton Tribune*, where he worked as a reporter and editor until 1982. His longest assignment at the newspaper was covering the federal courthouse (coincidentally, in the same building where I now work as a federal prosecutor). He became the *Tribune's* city editor in 1973.

In June 1969, 25 years after the D-Day landings, my father wrote a brief article summarizing some of his wartime experiences. At home, he rarely spoke about the war, and I never asked him detailed questions about his wartime service. He did show me some souvenirs he brought home from the war: a German soldier's helmet; a dagger; a canteen; and German coins. He stored those at my grandmother's house in Avoca.

My father also had a scrapbook which contained mostly photographs taken during the war; that, too, was stored in my grandmother's house. As a child, I looked through the scrapbook once or twice, but I never asked him about any of the photographs, nor did I understand the meaning and significance of the ribbons and medals therein. On a few occasions, usually when we were watching a war movie on television or the excellent television documentary *The World at War*, my father commented on something he recalled about the war. He mentioned how rough the sea was in the English Channel on June 6, 1944. He re-marked how difficult it was to climb down the rope ladder into the landing craft the next day as it approached the beach. He also mentioned the remarkable speed of the trucks that transported General Patton's troops and equipment eastward during the breakout after St Lo.

We had made plans to go to France in June 1984 to attend the 40th anniversary ceremonies of the Normandy invasion. But a few weeks before we were sche-duled to depart, my father suffered a broken leg, so we canceled the trip.

My father died of a heart attack on November 7, 1988, at the age of 72. Sever-al years prior to his death, after my grandmother died, we moved to his boyhood home in Avoca. A few years after his death, my sister, while searching for something in the basement, happened upon a shoebox stuffed with small enve-lopes. A closer look revealed that the envelopes contained letters that my father had written to his parents from Fort Meade, A.P. Hill, Camp Blanding, Camp Kilmer, England, France, and Germany from 1941 to 1945.

I read all of the letters—there were hundreds. Much of the content of the let-ters was about family matters, former co-workers, and friends back home in Avoca and Scranton. But the letters also provided snapshots of World War II as perceived and experienced by a combat soldier.

Reading the letters led me to do some research into the 29th Division's role in the Second World War. I read Joseph Ewing's *29 Lets Go*, an indispensable his-tory of the division; a War Department publication on the Battle of St Lo; Jo-seph Balkoski's trilogy on the 29th Division, *Omaha Beach, Beyond the Beach-head*, and *From Beachhead to Brittany*, and other books.

There was also much information on the internet, including "after action re-ports" and stories by or about other soldiers who served in the 29th Division during World War II.

I also looked more closely at my father's scrapbook. It included photographs of him and other soldiers at stateside forts, in England, and in France. It also had his ribbons and medals, including the Bronze Star along with the written citation accompanying the medal. The scrapbook also contained a news story in the *Scranton Tribune* about my father being drafted, a photograph of him riding in an army jeep being greeted by liberated French citizens (which appeared in the *Scranton Tribune*), and an article from the *Tribune* reporting on an interview with my father shortly after he returned home from the war.

With this material, I committed myself to writing about Frank Sempa's jour-ney through the Second World War. The result is this book.

This book is many things. First, it is a labor of love—my father was the great-est man I have ever known. Second, it is a tribute to his faithful and courageous service to his country during wartime. Third, it is a reminder to all Americans that the "greatest generation" is quickly dying out. Very few of the men who helped liberate parts of three continents remain with us. We must never forget them.

CHAPTER 2

Stateside Training

President Franklin Roosevelt, during his 1940 re-election campaign, promised the American people that he would not send their sons to fight in another war overseas. The United States, he said, would be the "arsenal of democracy," providing weapons, ships, and other assistance to Britain and France in their struggle with Nazi Germany.

In 1916, President Woodrow Wilson had made a similar pledge, and within a year the United States declared war on Germany and America's sons were being sent overseas to fight. Wilson's pledge was overtaken by events—Germany's policy of unrestricted submarine warfare, the consequent sinking of U.S. ships at sea, and the notorious Zimmerman Telegram in which Germany urged Mexico to join with it in a war against the United States.

FDR's pledge, too, was overtaken by events—Japan's surprise attack on the American fleet at Pearl Harbor and Hitler's subsequent declaration of war against the United States. FDR, like Wilson, would send America's sons overseas to fight.

Even before the 1940 election campaign, Roosevelt sensed that it would be difficult for the United States to stay out of the war in Europe or the Far East.

Germany had swiftly overrun Poland, occupied the Low Countries and defeated France, all in less than a year. The German air force was bombing British air-fields and cities in preparation for Operation "Sea Lion," the planned invasion of the British Isles.

Hitler's ally in Europe, Mussolini's Italy, had invaded and occupied parts of North Africa. Soviet Russia, meanwhile, had signed a non-aggression pact with Germany, invaded Finland, and invaded and occupied eastern Poland and the Baltic states.

Meanwhile, in the Far East, Japan had been on the march since the early 1930s, seizing parts of Manchuria, then invading and occupying coastal areas of China.

In these circumstances, it was only prudent to institute the Selective Service system to draft and train young American men to be soldiers in the event of war. After all, it was George Washington who wisely said that to be prepared for war was the best way to avoid war.

In April 1941, 24-year-old Frank Sempa was drafted into the U.S. Army. Born to John and Catherine Sempa of Avoca, Pennsylvania, on July 7, 1916, Frank Sempa attended elementary and secondary school in Avoca, earning good grades and never missing a day of school in 12 years.

He was the second of four sons, the youngest of whom would die at age 14 of a burst appendicitis. His father was an immigrant from Poland who worked as a coal miner.

At the time he was drafted into the army, my father worked as a correspondent for the *Scranton Tribune*. When he was drafted, an article appeared in the news-paper announcing that he was the first area newsman to be drafted. A photo-graph of my father accompanied the article. The pay, my father recalled, was $21 per month.[1]

My father and other draftees arrived at Fort Meade in April 1941. Fort Meade, named after the victorious Union commander at the Battle of Gettysburg, Gen-eral George G. Meade, was established in 1917 after the United States entered the First World War.

In the early spring of 1941, the fort consisted of dilapidated, unpainted bar-racks, some of which had no doors or windows, and mud—lots of mud. One of the 29th Division's officers described Fort Meade at that time as a "sea of mud."[2] My father recalled that when he arrived at Meade "the mud was ankle-deep," and some of the barracks were "unfinished."[3]

Prior to the arrival of the draftees, National Guard units from Virginia, Mary-land, Pennsylvania, and the District of Columbia—the nucleus of the 29th Divi-sion—were ordered to leave their state armories and assemble at Fort Meade. [4]

While at Meade, the structure of the 29th division evolved from two brigades, each with two infantry regiments and support units, to three infantry regiments and support units. The three infantry regiments that would eventually participate in the Normandy invasion and the liberation of France, Holland, and Germany were the 115th, the 116th, and my father's regiment—the 175th.

The soldiers of the 29th Division wore the distinctive circular blue and gray patch on the left shoulder of their uniforms. The "Blue and Gray" Division symbolized Northern and Southern solidarity in the U.S. Army. [5]

Stateside training for the 29th Division lasted from the spring of 1941 to September-October 1942, when the division was transported to England for more training in preparation for the invasion of Hitler's fortress Europe.

Using Meade as a base camp, the 29th Division held maneuvers and participated in war games at A.P. Hill Military Reservation near Fredericksburg, Virginia, and several locations in the Carolinas. In August 1942, the division's base camp shifted to Camp Blanding, Florida, with continued training and maneuvers at A.P. Hill and the Carolinas. My father later reflected that "this was the beginning of long preparations for battles . . . ."[6]

At Fort Meade in 1941, according to Joseph Ewing, "[i]t was a scorching summer for the new soldiers as they tramped, dusty and sweat-stained, over the . . . reservation." [7] The men of the 29th Division initially had little to do between drills. Later, the army arranged for USO shows and dances to keep the men occupied when they were not cleaning their guns and polishing their boots.

Initially, the men of the 29th Division trained with "dummy equipment."[8] After years of neglect, the army was experiencing growing problems, with frequent shortages of supplies. In one instance, my father's regiment, the 175th, had to give up its machine guns to the 115th regiment.[9]

Soldiers were afforded weekend passes, and used them to visit Washington, Baltimore, other towns in Maryland and Virginia, and to go home.

At A.P. Hill the conditions were more spartan. The men lived in tents instead of barracks. The food was worse and the men ate far less often. There were fewer weekend passes and furloughs. During maneuvers in North and South Carolina, the men were subjected to more realistic wartime conditions—sleeping in open fields in any weather; eating one meal a day; going for long time periods without sleep or food. The hikes were longer and the war games more intense. The new soldiers were learning "the new tactics and techniques of modern war."[10]

Joseph Ewing described the maneuvers as "great sprawling, rapidly moving affairs, with units scattered miles apart in the hills."[11] The soldiers of the 29th Division, wrote Ewing, "absorb[ed] the wet and cold of Carolina's autumn." [12]

By early December 1941, the division was on its way back to Fort Meade. When the Japanese attacked Pearl Harbor on December 7th, the soldiers of the 29th were spread out between A.P. Hill and South Boston, Virginia. My father remembered that his regiment "stopped for lunch in Virginia when the news of the Japanese attack on Pearl Harbor reached us via the airwaves . . . ."[13]

The onset of war meant practice blackouts and air raid precautions at Meade. My father's regiment continued to train for war and provided security to factories, railroad yards, bridges, warehouses, and other sites and facilities considered important to the war effort.[14]

In early 1942, the division got a new commander, Major General Leonard T. Gerow. That spring, the division moved to A.P. Hill to set up camp for another series of maneuvers. The men never returned to Meade. In mid-August 1942, the division moved to Camp Blanding, Florida.

On September 6, 1942, General Gerow announced that the division was moving north in preparation for overseas deployment. The men traveled by train to Camp Kilmer, New Jersey to await embarkation to England.

My father's letters during stateside training give some insight into how the army took young men from civilian life and molded them into combat soldiers. Stateside training involved boredom; long office hours doing paperwork; traveling hundreds of miles by jeep or truck on short notice; long hikes; sleeping in tents or out in the open in all kinds of weather; eating and drinking sparsely, if at all, during lengthy time periods; trudging through mud and snow on maneuvers; and going for days at a time without shaving, showering, or changing clothes.

In a letter to his brother Eddie, my father mentioned that "the going is tough," and noted that he was sleeping out in the open in terrible weather and eating once per day. In a letter written while he was riding on the back of a truck, my father informed his parents that he and the other soldiers get two quarts of water per day which is used for shaving, washing, and drinking.

Writing while on maneuvers in the woods of the Carolinas, my father noted that, "This week has been tough so far . . . ." He explained that it was "getting mighty cold out here . . . the nights are bitter." He said that he slept in a tent, there was heavy rain, and he got "soaked." On another occasion during war games, he wrote to his parents that he slept on the ground on "two blankets," and mentioned that he does not eat regularly because the food wagon cannot always break through "enemy" lines. He noted further that he had not had a shave or a change of clothes for five days.

In another letter from North Carolina, again written while riding on the back of a truck, my father explained that "we have been continuously on the go," without sleep and very little food.

Writing from Fort Meade after returning from weeklong maneuvers, my father told his parents that during maneuvers he did not shave, was awake all night, ate once every 24 hours, and was provided with one quart of water per day. The days, he wrote, are warm, but the nights are cold. "Sleeping out in the open is inconvenient at times," he noted, "but I'm getting use to it."

In several letters from A.P. Hill Military Reservation, my father described the mud as "disgusting." We are "always walking in two feet of it," he wrote. He referred to A.P. Hill as "God's forsaken country."

He described one night of maneuvers when he was with eight other soldiers in the woods at night with only a compass to guide them. "We didn't know where we were going," he wrote. He described "sliding down banks, falling into holes and trying to climb steep banks in the dark."

"[W]e've been out in the woods since early Sunday night," he wrote in a letter from South Carolina. "Rode in an open truck for over 40 miles—reaching our destination about 2:40am," he explained. "It was bitter cold," he noted, "and to top it all off we landed in Swampy Country . . . ." He described his dinner that evening as a "jam sandwich," and noted that "for the past three or four weeks all we have had for noonday lunch is a jam sandwich or two." He noted further that the bread was "hard." "Supper," he continued, "is usually hours late—in most instances we are fed in the dark so half the time we don't know what we are eating and we usually don't care." The coffee, he explained further, is "strong enough to talk back to you . . . ."

"[W]e are always on the move," he complained in another letter, and "it gets mighty tiresome but got to make the best of it."

In another letter from the field, my father told his parents that "the weather here is mighty hot," and he complained about "walking fourteen to sixteen miles per day with a full pack on your back." The soldiers "dropped out like flies," and he noted that he dropped out Monday afternoon and spent some time in a "clearing station hospital," but was now okay. "All we travel by is woods," he wrote, "and the roads are terribly dusty."

Writing from A.P. Hill, my father told his parents that it was the "coldest day of the year," and that there were four inches of snow on the ground. "Rode down in one of those jeeps," he wrote, "and almost froze." He explained that the jeep "has no top or sides on it." "We are living in tents," he noted, and "[e]ach tent has a stove in it and a wooden floor." The stove, he wrote, went out during the night. "Never dreamed it could be so cold in Virginia."

My father's letters are replete with references to attempts at securing weekend passes or furloughs. He frequently noted that he and the other soldiers visited nearby towns, such as Fredericksburg, to get a shave, a shower, or a good meal. In one letter, he described having a "very tasty" dinner consisting of chicken, mashed potatoes, peas, bread and butter, pudding, and ice cream. In another letter, he mentions eating a breakfast consisting of hot cakes, sausage, cereal, milk, and coffee.

He wrote to his parents about the wonderful hospitality shown to him and other soldiers by the people of the South. They "call you in off the street," he explained, "and give you everything they got." "The people here," he wrote, "are taking us in, feeding us, keeping us over the weekend and showing us a good time." "This Southern Hospitality," he noted, "is great. Never saw anything like it."

As his stateside training continued, my father was promoted to corporal, then to sergeant in Headquarters Company of the 175th regiment. He noted in his letters that he was frequently "put in charge" of the company" when the First Sergeant was away. He told his parents that he often spent long days and nights working in the company office.

The letters also reveal that my father was adjusting well to military life and gaining confidence in his leadership abilities. "I have been in charge here all week," he wrote in one letter. "That leaves me the boss of everything. I tell them all what to do and when to do it. All orders must come from me." He expressed confidence that he could handle the job of First Sergeant, and speculated that he might be offered that position.

He also made sure, however, that when he was put in charge of the company, he saw to the men's morale. In one letter he noted that he was in charge for the next ten days which meant "we are going to have a company party."

My father's battalion (3rd Battalion of the 175th), he noted in a letter, was selected to give a demonstration at Fort Belvoir, Virginia, to several congressmen and Vice President Henry Wallace. The demonstration, he noted with obvious pride, "was a great success."

Shortly after the attack on Pearl Harbor, while at Fort Meade, my father wrote to his parents that he "[r]eceived the war news while in Virginia." "There is nothing new on it in camp," he wrote, "but high ranking officials of our division are of the opinion that our division will not be called upon to fight as it will be a naval and air fight against Japan." "Please don't worry about me," he wrote, "for God is good and I think everything will turn out for the best." In an obvious effort to calm his parents, he wrote, "While clouds are black there is bound to be a silver lining so all we can do is hope and pray that it ends soon." He noted that "[i]t is surprising how calmly the men in camp are taking the war." He added, "We will all have to be good soldiers."

In another letter in which my father obviously tried to calm the fears of his parents about the war, he wrote, "There is not much room for the infantry in this war and I believe it will be fought greatly in the air and on the sea."

My father was clearly adjusting well to army life, including the growing prospect of overseas deployment. "[T]his army is built on traveling," he wrote, "and I enjoy it. Might just as well see as much of this world as possible while the army is paying for it."

In a July 1942 letter, he informed his parents that Camp Blanding in Florida would be his next base camp. "I don't expect we will stay there long," he wrote, "and it wouldn't surprise me a bit to see us in some foreign country before the year is out." "That's O.K. by me," he wrote. "Let's get into this thing and get it over with." In a subsequent letter, he predicted that the division would probably be shipped to England.

After arriving at Camp Blanding in August 1942, my father wrote to his parents, describing the new camp as "beautiful . . . much nicer than Meade." He noted that unlike Meade, Camp Blanding had swimming, theaters, canteens and service clubs. At Blanding, there was more and better equipment. The nation was gearing-up for total war.

My father also informed his parents that he had been a witness at two courts martial where soldiers were fined $80 for being AWOL for ten days.

My father's last stateside letters were sent from Camp Kilmer, New Jersey. On

October 6, 1942, he told his parents to "Take good care of yourselves and if you don't hear from me in some length of time don't worry its just that we are on the go and are either unable or haven't the time to write."

The previous day, October 5, 1942, my father and his regiment embarked on the *Queen Elizabeth* for England and the second part of his journey through the Second World War.

NOTES

1. Frank F. Sempa, "First Area Newsman to be Drafted Recalls Horror of Omaha Beach," *Scranton Tribune*, June 1, 1969.

2. Joseph Balkoski, *Beyond the Beachhead: The 29th Infantry Division in Normandy* (Mechanicsburg, PA: Stackpole Books, 1999), p. 19.

3. Sempa, *Scranton Tribune*, June 1, 1969.

4. Joseph H. Ewing, *29 Let's Go: A History of the 29th Infantry Division in World War II* (Washington, D.C.: Infantry Journal Press, 1948), p. 1.

5. Balkoski, *Beyond the Beachhead*, p. 25.

6. Sempa, *Scranton Tribune*, June 1, 1969.

7. Ewing, *29 Let's Go*, p. 3.

8. Ewing, *29 Let's Go*, p. 2.

9. Edwin P. Hoyte, *The GI's War: American Soldiers in Europe During world War II* (New York: De Capo Press 1988), p. 41.

10. Ewing, *29 Let's Go*, p. 2.

11. Ewing, *29 Let's Go*, p. 7.

12. Ewing, *29 Let's Go*, p. 7.

13. Sempa, *Scranton Tribune*, June 1, 1969.

14. Ewing, *29 Let's Go*, p. 8; Sempa, *Scranton Tribune*, June 1, 1969.

CHAPTER 3

England

In one of his first letters from England, my father described the trip across the Atlantic Ocean as "uneventful." The *Queen Elizabeth*, carrying about 15,000 troops, cruised to the United Kingdom at 28 knots, turning and zig-zagging frequently to avoid German U-boats.[1] The Battle of the Atlantic was still raging at the time, and the U-boat menace was real and potentially deadly.

My father's regiment landed in Scotland at the Firth of Clyde on October 11, 1942, after a "five-day journey across the Atlantic."[2] One of the first things American soldiers noticed was the numerous barrage balloons designed to protect against air attack. Although the Royal Air Force had won the Battle of Britain over the skies of the United Kingdom and the English Channel, German air attacks continued. I recall my father telling me that after the huge build-up of American forces and equipment in England, he and other soldiers used to joke that the only things preventing the island from sinking were the ubiquitous barrage balloons.

The 29th was the second U.S. infantry division to arrive in England. The 1st Division had trained there in preparation for the landings in North Africa.[3] My father's regiment was transported by train from Scotland to southern England, settling in at Tidworth Barracks, an old British cavalry post near Andover and Salisbury, a short distance from Stonehenge. What my father and the other soldiers in his division saw during the train ride was, in Joseph Ewing's words, "England's autumn landscape." Ewing described this as "[m]ile after mile of rolling hills, bluish with heather, honey-combed with endless stone fences . . . [c]rooked country lanes, stone cottages [and] dinky four-wheeled 'goods wagons.'"[4]

On October 13, 1942, my father wrote his first letter to his parents from England. He mentioned that he had sent a telegram informing them of his safe arrival there. The people of England, he wrote, are treating the Americans well so far. He immediately recognized what Winston Churchill had called the indomitable spirit of the British nation. "Being in England," my father wrote, "gives one a better conception of what these brave people have gone through. Despite all of their hardships they sure do have spirit." He told his parents not to worry about him and asked them to send him razor blades and candy. "In my opinion," he boldly remarked, "this war will be of short duration for nothing will stop us once we get going."

Five days later, my father attempted to allay the fears of his parents-- something he did throughout his journey through the Second World War--by opining that, "this struggle is not going to last much longer. Why one of these days we're liable to wake up and find this whole mess is over." He repeated these sentiments in a letter dated October 31, 1942. "Who knows," he wrote, "but that this war will soon be over and we'll all be home once again to start life all over again."

On October 24, 1942, my father sent his first V-mail letter to his parents. V-mail was a four-inch by five-inch piece of paper on which soldiers typed, wrote, or printed letters. At the top of the paper, from left to right, was the army censor's stamp, the person or persons to whom the letter was sent and an address, and the return address of the sender. While my father was overseas, his return address was "Hq Co 175th Inf Reg Apo 29, c/o NY NY," and then the date was noted below. Soldiers were encouraged to use V-mail to save paper--most of my father's letters were written on V-mail.

While it saved paper, using V-mail limited the number of words in each letter. My father and other soldiers had only four-by-four inches of paper on which to write, print, or type, and they used every inch of it.

Within two weeks after arriving in England, my father and his regiment took a week-long course on chemical warfare. "Monday," he wrote on October 27, 1942, "I started chemical warfare school . . . I enjoyed the sessions, learning something new everyday." He explained that "the school is to last but one week and I wish it were more for I really am interested in it." In the First World War, both sides used poison gas and it was anticipated that chemical warfare would be used again in this war. It was only prudent, therefore, to educate our soldiers about this deadly form of warfare.

Chemical warfare school was merely a part of what Joseph Ewing described as a grueling seven-day per week training program. This training included two 25-mile hikes per week. My father mentioned taking a 25-mile hike in a November 22, 1942 letter, and in another letter he informed his parents that the hikes "toughen one up." "Men who were physically unable to complete the march were . . . transferred," Ewing noted.[5] Balkoski's research confirmed this. "Anyone who couldn't meet the rigorous training standards," he wrote, "was transferred . . . out of the division. Some companies . . . lost almost fifty percent of their men during the division's training period in England."[6] My father met those rigorous training standards.

On October 29, my father wrote to his brother John that "everything with me over here in England is ok." He noted that he had put in for "Officers Candidate School" because "being over here in the actual war zone gives one a better conception of things." "This war," he opined, will "last a few years." He mentioned that he might decide to make a career out of the army.

Much of the 29th Division's training took place on the moors of southwest England, near Devon, Cornwall, Torquay, and Exeter. The moors were described as "broad stretches of barren terrain, utterly desolate, covered with spongy grass, occasional shrubs, prickly evergreen, and outcropping rock."[7] The war games on the moors were designed to acquaint the men with the "sites and sounds of battle so they could learn to overcome panic when they were under fire."[8]

In addition to the desolate training grounds, the soldiers of the 29th Division hiked, marched, and trained in dismal weather. Rain, drizzle, fog, and sodden ground were the norm. My father's letters are replete with references to rain and miserable weather.

Life for an American soldier in England, however, was not all work. There were passes and furloughs that enabled soldiers of the 29th to visit British towns and cities. On November 19, 1942, my father wrote that he spent Saturday and Sunday "on pass visiting a nearby town." He also noted that he spent two days in London. "Let me tell you," he wrote, "it is quite a city. I enjoyed the visit very much. The beautiful historic buildings are something to admire. It sure was a fine trip." He noted that he was "looking to visit [London] again in the near future."

On December 19, 1942, my father had to undergo appendicitis surgery in an English hospital. He first mentioned this in a letter to his parents on Christmas Day. He told them that he came out of the surgery fine, was in no pain, received great treatment, and noted that the nurses were great. In a subsequent letter, he noted that some of the nurses who took care of him were from Texas and New Jersey.

In that same Christmas Day letter, my father expressed to his parents the "hope that you are enjoying this Christmas Day." The soldiers in his company, he noted, were enjoying Christmas "over here." "It is a beautiful day," he noted, "with the sun shining brightly. Of course, we would have liked a few inches of snow but as it is we are well satisfied." He expressed confidence that "next X-mas shall find us back in the states. This war is going to be over sooner than you . . . expect."

My father, an observant Catholic all of his life, also assured his parents that he went to Confession and Communion that morning. He also described his Christmas dinner: tomato juice, celery, pickles, roast turkey with dressing, cranberry sauce, mashed potatoes, peas, salad, hot rolls and butter, plum pudding, coffee, cookies, and fruit cake. "We really had a fine X-mas over here," he concluded, "and the English did everything possible to make it the best."

Three days later, perhaps carried away by the holiday spirit, or just trying to calm the fears of his parents, my father wrote that, "Everyone over here is so optimistic that the European war will end in 1943."

In a letter written on New Year's Eve, he noted the end of another year, and that he spent a "quiet" New Year's Eve, "nothing like back in the states."

The next day, January 1, 1943, my father told his parents that "Our X-mas celebration was quiet as was the New Year. Nothing like the good old times in the U.S.A." He noted that almost everything in England was rationed due to the war, and that he goes to the Red Cross for a "coke and a hamburger." He remarked that "the war news sure does look good and I think the war will end this year."

The Red Cross set up Tidworth House near Tidworth Barracks to entertain American soldiers. Located in the Duke of Wellington's mansion, the Red Cross club enabled my father and other U.S. servicemen to enjoy a touch of America while training for war in England. Red Cross clubs were established throughout England so that soldiers could enjoy movies, shows, coca colas and hamburgers. Indeed, in one letter my father noted that "the Red Cross is the only place you can get cokes and American hamburgers."

In many letters from England, my father mentioned being at the Red Cross to see a movie or a show, or to attend a dance. In a January 12, 1943 letter, he told his parents that he saw "Abbott and Costello in 'Ride 'm Cowboy'" the previous night "and it was good." In a subsequent letter in March 1943, he noted that while he was at the Red Cross he "saw a movie, heard some good entertainment and had three cokes and a like number of hamburgers."

He repeatedly praised the work of the Red Cross. The following comment in one of his letters is typical: "The Red Cross is a mighty fine organization and they have been doing wonderful work over here." I also recall him telling me many years later that the Salvation Army did a great job of caring for American soldiers during the war.

In February 1943, my father visited London again, remarking in a letter that he saw "Westminster Abbey, Buckingham Palace, [the] House of Parliament, and other great buildings . . . ." That same month, he told his parents that he had an "Irish girlfriend" in London and had been to visit her. Apparently, she was not the only one.

In a letter written on February 10, 1943, my father told his parents that "Everything with me over here is fine and dandy and I am feeling fine." He met, he wrote, "a dozen or two interesting girls over here." He noted that he was dating several of them and remarked that the "only trouble with those dates are that you have to return so early. . ." He wrote that he was going to "shave, shine my shoes, put on my clean clothes, and get ready for a date. She's Irish and lovely. Who knows but that I might bring back with me a half-dozen or so of these gals from over here."

In a subsequent letter in July 1943, my father noted that "[t]he English girls are treating me fine." "Already," he continued, "I have a dozen that want me to take them back to the states." In another letter he noted that he was dating a "charming blonde" that he met while on a pass. He described her as "gorgeous" and "the most charming blonde I have ever seen."

Along with girls, American servicemen in England enjoyed playing sports. In a February 27, 1943 letter, my father noted that the weather was improving "and we are beginning to play baseball." In other letters that year he mentioned playing softball and football.

There were other recreational activities for soldiers, too. In a July 5, 1943 letter, my father noted that he had been on a pass over the weekend at "one of England's finest summer resorts." He "did some horseback riding, swimming, and hiking among other things." The weather, he noted, "was simply wonderful."

Wonderful weather, however, was not the norm. In letter after letter, my father complained about the rain and the terrible English weather. He also complained about English beer. In a March 10, 1943 letter, my father wrote, "We can't get any American beer over here and I don't like the English beer at all." In a letter written in April 1943, my father reiterated to his parents that "the beer over here is terrible. I never touch it." In October 1943, my father wrote that "[i]t sure will be a relief to get back to the states for a good glass of beer among other things."

During his stay in England my father did become accustomed to English tea. In July 1943, he noted in letters that he was having a "spot of tea," and was becoming "Englishized" in that regard. In a subsequent letter, he remarked that he was getting to be "quite a tea drinker."

Food, too, was an important part of life in England for the American soldiers. My father's letters are replete with detailed references to meals that he especially enjoyed. In June 1943, my father mentioned eating "fresh strawberries" and "fresh eggs," and "a lot of vegetables." In July 1943, he mentioned eating fresh eggs again, noting that they were hard to get in England. In August 1943, he informed his parents that he had ice cream for the first time in England. In October 1943, he remarked that he had an orange for the first time since leaving the states. That same month he noted that while on pass he had "fresh eggs, bacon, and toast each morning, just as though I were back home."

In a February 25, 1944 letter, my father mentioned that he had just finished supper which consisted of "roast beef, gravy, potatoes, peas, cole slaw, peaches, and coffee . . . ." In March 1944, he mentioned getting fresh eggs for breakfast, along with "hot cakes and sausage." He explained that "our food of late has been very good; plenty of steak, pork chops, chicken, etc., and pie and cake." The food, it seems, was getting better the closer it got to D-Day.

Mail from home was very important for the morale of the American soldiers in England. My father frequently mentioned in his letters to his parents that he received letters and packages from friends and former co-workers at the *Scranton Tribune*. He also mentioned, with much gratitude, the letters and packages he received from his parents.

Those packages often contained candy and other non-perishable goods that brought great joy to my father, judging from his letters. They also included razors, pens, pencils, and other practical items. He always made sure to express his gratitude to his parents for making his stay in England a little more pleasant.

The letters from his parents allowed my father to stay informed on the people and events back home in Avoca and Scranton. In virtually every letter, my father comments on some bit of news that his parents mentioned in their letters. Who was getting married? Who was getting divorced? Who was in the hospital? What were his brothers Eddie and John up to? Who got a new job? Who lost a job?

My father also stayed in touch with events back home by receiving by mail copies of the *Scranton Tribune*. In his letters, he invariably mentions the number of *Tribunes* he received in the mail--they usually came in bunches. He frequently commented on a particular news item that he read in the newspaper.

He also made sure to praise the news items in the *Tribune* written by his mother. When my father was inducted into the army, his mother assumed his duties as a local correspondent for the *Tribune*. She wrote about, as he did before being drafted, events in Avoca and surrounding communities. It was my father's intention, as he noted in a few letters, to resume his correspondent job with the *Tribune* if and when he returned home from the war.

Based on the description of the contents of my father's letters thus far, it could appear that my father wrote only about himself and his situation in England. The theme and purpose of this book is to describe a combat soldier's journey through the Second World War, so naturally I have focused on his experiences and what he wrote about himself. But his letters to his parents show a constant concern for their well-being.

The letters reflect that my father consistently sent money home, some of it in the form of bonds, to assist his parents financially. He told them several times to use the bonds whenever they needed them. He constantly asked them if they needed him to send more money home. He also repeatedly inquired about their health, and did everything possible to allay their fears about the hazards he faced and would face in war. The phrases "don't worry about me" and "I am fine" appear again and again in my father's letters.

In his letters, he was the eternal optimist. As noted previously, shortly after he arrived in England, he wrote to his parents that "this struggle is not going to last much longer. Why one of these days we're liable to wake up and find this whole mess is over." During Christmas 1942, he remarked that "we are all confident that next X-mas shall find us back in the states. This war is going to be over sooner than you people expect." On New Years Day 1943, he opined that the war would end that year. In a July 1943 letter, my father wrote that "War news sure does look better with each passing day. Who knows but that the end is in sight." In a Christmas Eve letter in 1943, he predicted to his parents that "we will all be home by next year at this time."

In the spring of 1943, the 29th Division moved to Devon, Cornwall, Torquay and Exeter, and took over responsibility for the defense of part of the southern coast of England. The 175th regiment participated in "Operation Columbus," a three-day tactical maneuver.[9]

In July 1943, the division got a new commander, Major General Charles H. Gerhardt. According to Balkoski, Gerhardt was a strict disciplinarian who visited the men frequently and infused a spirit of aggressiveness in the division.[10]

In late May and early June 1943, my father and the other soldiers in the division began training for amphibious assaults. The beaches in England chosen for the training were Slapton Sands and Woolacombe because of their similarity to the beaches at Normandy.[11] The training included climbing down cargo nets, storming beaches, waterproofing vehicles, and swimming. The division had to learn how to assemble, approach, attack, and defend under the most hazardous of circumstances. Although the men of the 29th Division did not know it, this was specific training for D-Day.

In his letters written at this time, viewed in hindsight, my father hints at more intensive training. On May 30, 1943, my father noted in a letter that he "spent several days out in the field and came in late last night very tired." On June 18, 1943, my father informed his parents that they had moved to another part of England, and that he was spending a lot of time "in the field." Two days later he again mentioned the move, and remarked that next week will be a busy one. In a June 25, 1943 letter, he noted that he was "out in the field," had a nasty sunburn, and would not be able to wash for a few days.

Prior to the initial training in amphibious warfare, members of my father's regiment were granted furloughs. On June 17, 1943, my father wrote that he had just returned from a six-day furlough to London. He mentioned meeting soldiers from many other countries of Europe, including Poland, France, Norway, and Czechoslovakia.

After the training, there was time for some fun and relaxation. In fact, in a letter dated July 15, 1943, my father wrote, "This afternoon I saw Bob Hope in person and he sure did present an excellent show." My father said that he "[l]aughed for a continuous 45 minutes."

The war news, of course, was on everyone's mind. In January 1943, my father mentioned in a letter reading about a soldier from back home who was killed in North Africa. "Such are the fortunes of war," he wrote. In a May 10, 1943 letter, my father mentioned that there was good news on the African front. He obviously was referring to the impending surrender of Axis forces in North Africa which occurred three days later.

More good news came on September 8, 1943, when Italy surrendered to the Allies. The Italian peninsula, according to British Prime Minister Winston Churchill and his military advisers, was the "soft underbelly" of Europe. After the Allied victory in North Africa, Churchill persuaded President Roosevelt to ignore the advice of his principal military advisers and to invade Italy next, and put off the planned invasion of France.

The Italian campaign, however, proved to be anything but soft. Allied forces had to slug their way up the Italian boot against tough German resistance, making famous such places as Anzio, Salerno, and Monte Cassino. Italy's surrender, though welcome, did not mean the end of the fighting because German forces effectively occupied and defended the country.

In a letter to his parents dated September 8, 1943, my father wrote, "Just heard of the unconditional surrender of Italy. Seems to me it is the beginning of the end." Two days later, he wrote, "Guess you people are rejoicing over the surrender of Italy. It won't be long now before its all over."

In some of his letters from England, my father reflected on the length of time he had been in the army or away from home. On April 25, 1943, my father noted his second anniversary in the army. "The years have passed quickly," he wrote, "and I hope the remainder of my time in the service passes as quickly." A month later, he noted that "[i]t's 25 months today since I entered the army. Time sure does pass, does it not?" On October 2, 1943, he wrote that its "been a little more than a year since I was home. . . Maybe a year from now we will be home again." On April 12, 1944, he wrote that "its three years this month the army got me. Sure does seem like a long time but it has passed rather quickly." On April 24, 1944, he recalled that "it was three years ago that the Army gave me a uniform." The next day he wrote that "it was three years ago tomorrow that I first found out what an Army uniform looked like! Who'd ever think 3 years ago that we would be in that long!"

In September 1943, the army established the Assault Training Center to begin final training for "Operation Overlord," the invasion of the Normandy beaches in France. In the late fall of 1943 through the early winter of 1944, the Allies planned amphibious assault training exercises. In late December 1943 to early January 1944, the 29th Division participated in Exercise Duck also known as Duck I at Slapton Sands beaches. This was a rehearsal for the D-Day landings that were now planned for May or June 1944. It was "a full-scale amphibious exercise involving the closest coordination with the Navy, air force, and Services of Supply . . . ."[12] The troops used the same ports of embarkation that would be used in the invasion. The goal was to duplicate as much as possible in a training exercise the actual conditions of embarkation, approach, and assault. "While destroyers and cruisers hammered simulated German pillboxes with live shells," explained Joseph Balkoski, "the men slithered and crawled along the sands, blowing gaps in barbed wire and firing their rifles into the coastal dunes."[13] The soldiers trained using flame-throwers, bangalore torpedoes, and bazookas.[14]

In a post-war manuscript, the army's historical division called "Duck 1" the first and "probably the most important" exercise for the Normandy invasion. It had two phases: first, assembling, processing, and embarking troops; and second, the actual assault. More than 10,000 troops participated in the exercise, including my father's regiment. Observers critiqued the exercise, noting that the landings did not go as planned, the landing craft commanders did not breach at the proper points, pre-invasion security was bad, signal communications was hampered by lack of equipment, and there was a significant lack of coordination between the Army and Navy.[15]

Subsequent exercises, code-named Duck II, Duck III, Fox, Tiger, and Fabius were held during February through May 1944. Fabius attempted to duplicate, as much as possible, the conditions expected on the Normandy beaches and involved more than 25,000 troops.[16]

My father's letters during this time provided subtle hints that he was involved in something militarily significant and highly classified. On October 9, 1943, he told his parents that "there is lots that I could write about but far be it from me to step on the censor's toes." He indicated that he would not be able to tell them anything "until this mess is all over." Two days later, he wrote, "there is lots to write about but it would come under military information so it will have to wait." In a December 16, 1943 letter, my father mentioned that he had a "busy day . . . but a very interesting one. Too bad military censorship prevents me from saying something about it." On January 21, 1944, he attempted to explain to his parents why they had not heard from him lately. "I have been out in the field," he wrote. "I returned today and am tired." Ten days later, he wrote that "we are still out in the field," it was 2:00am, and he still had work to do.

On February 7, 1944, my father again explained in a letter that he did not write any mail between December 25 and January 7 "because I wasn't in a position to."

Joseph Balkoski in *Beyond the Beachhead*, noted that in January 1944, British General Bernard Montgomery, who would play a key role in Operation Overlord, visited the 29th Division.[17] My father told his parents about this in a letter dated January 15, 1944. "Today," he wrote, "I saw General Montgomery. He sure is a fine man and has a swell personality. Now I understand why he was such a success in Africa and Italy."

Christmas 1943 was mostly spent training for war, but my father managed to get a letter out to his parents on Christmas Eve and Christmas Day. On Christmas Eve he wrote, "Well here it is the night before X-mas. Got me to thinking about such evenings at home." "Tomorrow," he wrote, "will be just another day but I'm sure we will be home by next year at this time . . . ." "They sure are keeping us busy these days," he wrote.

In his Christmas Day letter he wrote, "No doubt at this time . . . you're enjoying your X-mas turkey dinner." He mentioned that the troops had turkey for dinner, too. "Only thing I missed was the X-mas tree," he wrote. He told them that he went to church in the morning, but "have been working the remainder of the day." "You know," he wrote, "this is no time for play. Want to get this thing over with and get back home."

Between February 10-17, 1944, my father was on furlough in Scotland. "Had a swell time," he wrote on February 18, 1944. "The Scotch people are mighty fine." He noted that he just returned and was "well rested and in a much better frame of mind." "I needed the rest," he explained.

On April 6, 1944, my father expressed to his parents the wish that "this mess would end and we could get home." Three days later he wrote, "I guess that guy who said the war would end today was a bit premature." On April 12, 1944, my father wrote to his brother John. "Remember," he said, "I'm depending on you to keep things at home under control if anything should happen to me." On May 1, 1944, my father responded to some minor concern of his parents by writing, "I have too many big things on my mind to be worried by trivial matters."

In mid May, the entire 29th Division was "pulled out of its encampments . . . and moved to special assembly areas on the coast near Plymouth and Falmouth."[18] The assembly areas were surrounded by barbed wire and guarded by counterintelligence personnel.[19] "No unauthorized personnel were permitted to leave or enter and camouflage discipline was strictly enforced."[20] In several letters written in late May 1944, my father mentioned that he is being kept "busy," but there is no hint that something very momentous was afoot. He later recalled that "the call came to get ready for the greatest battle of our lives."[21]

Shortly before D-Day, General Omar Bradley, the commander of the First U.S. Army, visited the 29th Division. "This stuff about tremendous losses," he said, "is tommyrot. Some of you won't come back, but it'll be very few." Bradley told the men that they should consider themselves lucky because "You're going to have ringside seats for the greatest show on earth."[22]

My father's journey through the Second World War was entering a new, more dangerous, and more historic phase. The "big things" he referred to in his May 1st letter were about to begin. He and his division were about to embark, with others, on an historic mission to help liberate the continent of Europe.

NOTES

1. Balkoski, *Beyond the Beachhead*, p. 36.
2. Sempa, *Scranton Tribune*, June 1, 1969.
3. Ewing, *29 Let's Go*, pp. 15-17.
4. Ewing, *29 Let's Go*, p. 15.
5. Ewing, *29 Let's Go*, p. 16.
6. Balkoski, *Beyond the Beachhead*, p. 54.
7. Ewing, *29 Let's Go*, p. 21.
8. Balkoski, *Beyond the Beachhead*, p. 52.
9. Ewing, *29Let's Go*, p. 20.
10. Balkoski, *Beyond the Beachhead*, p. 51.
11. Ewing, *29 Let's Go*, p. 22.
12. Ewing, *29 Let's Go*, p. 27.
13. Balkoski, *Beyond the Beachhead*, p. 57.
14. Michael Reynolds, *Eagles and Bulldogs in Normandy 1944* (Havertown, PA: Casemate 2003), p. 4.
15. Clifford L. Jones, "Neptune: Training, Mounting, the Artificial Ports," Historical Division, U.S. Army Forces, European Theatre, March 1946, www.history.army.mil/documents/wwii/beaches/bchs-7.htm.
16. Jones, "Neptune: Training, mounting, the Artificial Ports."
17. Balkoski, *Beyond the Beachhead*, p. 58.
18. Balkoski, *Beyond the Beachhead*, p. 60.
19. Reynolds, *Eagles and Bulldogs*, p. 5.
20. Reynolds, *Eagles and Bulldogs*, p. 5.
21. Sempa, *Scranton Tribune*, June 1, 1969.

22. Reynolds, *Eagles and Bulldogs*, p. 6.

CHAPTER 4

Somewhere in France

OMAHA BEACH

The 29th Division's mission in the D-Day landings on June 6, 1944, was to assault Omaha Beach on the Normandy coast of France, establish a secure beachhead, and move as far inland as logistically possible while linking-up with American forces invading Utah Beach. During the early morning hours of June 6th, Allied airborne forces parachuted and glided behind enemy lines in Normandy to cause confusion and upset German reinforcement efforts. In the days and months leading up to the invasion, Allied bombers targeted the transportation infrastructure of the French countryside and the military emplacements of the Atlantic Wall. An elaborate deception plan persuaded key members of the German High Command that Calais, not Normandy, was the main target of the Allied invasion.

Meanwhile, a great armada of Allied warships embarked from coastal areas of England, traversed the rough seas of the English Channel, pounded the bluffs overlooking the beaches with naval gunfire, and delivered the invading infantry regiments to the beach approaches.

The initial assault on Omaha Beach was made by the 1st Division and the 29th Division's 116th infantry regiment. Almost nothing went as planned. The air and naval bombardment had not knocked-out many German bunkers and pillboxes that overlooked the beach. As a result, the men in the initial assault waves were subjected to murderous machine-gun and artillery fire. Many soldiers were killed before they could exit the landing craft. Others jumped over the sides of the boats into the rough seas to their deaths. Some landing craft struck mines resulting in many dead and wounded soldiers. Some troops landed in the wrong place.

Once ashore, the invading forces suffered horrendous casualties in their efforts to penetrate German defenses. In many instances, the command structure broke down as officers and company commanders repeatedly fell to enemy fire. Many soldiers reached the beach and started digging in often futile attempts to avoid the concentrated German machine-gun and artillery fire.

The topography of Omaha Beach was such that the goal of the invading Americans was to push through the natural pathways or "draws" in the bluffs and cliffs behind the beach. These "draws" were heavily defended by mines, barbed wire, and machine-gun nests. U.S. troops used bangalore torpedoes to blow holes in the barbed wire and open the draws to assault and exploitation.

The 29th Division's 115th regiment landed on Omaha Beach in the second wave during the late morning hours of June 6th. One 29th Division officer recalled that "nothing can approach the scenes on the beach from 1130 to 1400 hours: men being killed like flies from unseen gun positions."[1] By day's end, American forces at Omaha Beach, at great cost, had established a thin and precarious beachhead. Chester Wilmot described the American penetration at Omaha Beach as "slight and insecure."[2] No D-Day objectives had been reached. Fifty landing craft and ten larger vehicles were lost. About 3,000 U.S. troops had been killed, wounded or missing, including more than 1,000 casualties in the 29th Division's 116th regiment alone. That heroic regiment earned 23 Distinguished Service Crosses, 10 Silver Stars, and 100 Bronze Stars for its actions on D-Day.[3]

"As D-Day came to an end," writes historian John C. McManus, "the situation was fluid." Instead of an established front line, McManus explains, "there were clusters of Americans and Germans--dug in, patrolling, skirmishing, existing--in close proximity to one another all along the coastline."[4]

"When darkness settled over Omaha," writes Balkoski, "the flames of burning landing craft shed an eerie, dancing light, silhouetting the living and the dead on the beach. Those who walked along the sand that night had to be careful to avoid stepping on corpses."[5]

My father's regiment, the 175th, spent D-Day at sea in reserve waiting to exploit whatever inroads were made by the first day's assault. Shortly before noon on June 7, 1944 (D-Day +1), the 175th Infantry was ordered to begin landing on Omaha Beach. The 175th, like all U.S. Infantry regiments, was composed of three battalions: the 1st, 2nd, and 3rd. Each battalion, which totaled about 930 men, had four companies, including a headquarters company.[6]

The battalions and companies of the 175th were notified by small navy motorboats using loudspeakers to go ashore: "All elements of the 175th Infantry urgently needed on the beach." Soldiers exited their respective transport ships by climbing down cargo nets into the landing craft that would take them to the beach. I recall my father mentioning to me that the sea was very rough and it was difficult maneuvering down the cargo nets into the landing craft.

The area immediately offshore Omaha Beach was a scene of mass confusion. It was "almost as chaotic as . . . on the beach itself."[7] That fact, combined with rough seas, separate transport ships and landing craft, and the separate notification to land by small boats meant that "the 175th set out piecemeal for the beach."[8] The regiment landed piecemeal, too, "with no real command and control."[9]

My father's regiment stormed ashore near les Moulins draw between 12:30pm and 4:00pm.[10] Two of the landing craft struck mines and were destroyed. My father and most of the other soldiers of the regiment landed safely and quickly moved to the seawall. They were under intermittent machine-gun and artillery fire from some German defenders who had not been cleared from the bluffs the previous day.

No one who was on Omaha Beach the day after D-Day would ever forget what they saw. Tanks were burning. Boats were wrecked. Worst of all, the bodies of dead Americans, many wearing the blue and gray patch of the 29th Division, were visible on the beach and rolling back and forth in the wave surge. A captain in the 175th described it as looking like "something out of Dante's Inferno."[11] My father later recalled that "death was everywhere on Omaha Beach. In seconds [after landing] you realized that war is hell."[12]

General Gerhardt had wanted the 175th to land opposite the Vierville draw and swiftly move inland. Instead, the navy landed the regiment opposite the les Moulins draw, more than a mile east of where it was supposed to land. This meant "a long cross movement of the beach by the entire regiment."[13] The regiment's After Action Report noted that the move across the beach to Vierville encountered "occasional mortar and machine gun fire."[14]

As my father's regiment walked across the beach, the men stepped over the bodies of the soldiers of the 116th and 115th regiments who did not make it off the beach on D-Day. The 175th marched "in a column of battalions": 1st, 2nd, and 3rd (my father's) to Gruchy. Its first field order was to "Advance from assembly area, seize and hold Isigny with the least practicable delay."[15]

NORMANDY BEACHHEAD

The 29th Division marched to Gruchy and along the way it had to "wipe out small pockets of enemy resistance and snipers."[16] My father's regiment moved into Gruchy by about 8:00pm, and the headquarters of my father's battalion was hit by a concentration of German shells, resulting in casualties.[17] This tough enemy resistance convinced the division's high command to reinforce the 175th with the 747th Tank Battalion.[18]

At approximately 9:30pm on June 7, my father's regiment, with tanks leading the way, moved along "the . . . road . . . to la Cambe."[19]During the early morning hours of June 8, the 175th rested for a few hours near the Formigny-Isigny Road. After resuming its march, the regiment moved into la Cambe where it encountered little enemy resistance but came under fire from Allied war planes.[20] The 175th suffered six killed and several more wounded as a result of this friendly fire incident.[21]

Southwest of la Cambe, my father's regiment engaged in heavy fighting with German infantry armed with 88mm guns at St. Germaine du Pert. The After Action Report notes that this German "strong point was reduced and driven back after heavy fighting" by about 4:00pm.[22] "The 3rd Battalion," writes John McManus, "pushed the German defenders of St-Germaine-du-Pert south, all the way across the flooded Aure River."[23] My father, in his article written 25 years after D-Day, recalled fighting at St Germaine du Pert.

Meanwhile, the 175th's other two battalions took nearby Osmanville and Cardonville.[24] Shortly after midnight, on June 9, elements of the 175th were within 500 meters of Isigny. The 747th Tank Battalion led the way to Isigny, followed closely by my father's battalion and the 1st battalion.

At about 3:00am, wrote Joseph Ewing, "[t]he leading tanks, firing their machine guns and cannon, entered the city, which was blazing in the fires that had been started by naval guns and air attacks."[25] The 29th Division's After Action Report notes that the Ninth Army Air Force "was to bomb ISIGNY with incendiary bombs prior to the attack of the 175th Inf."[26]

The town of Isigny had been reduced by U.S. air and naval power to burning buildings and rubble. When my father's regiment entered the town, the troops were harassed by sniper fire, but tanks and bazookas quickly ended that threat. The 175th took 200 German prisoners.

Historian Michael Reynolds calls the capture of Isigny by my father's regiment a "remarkable achievement." "In less than thirty-six hours after coming ashore on OMAHA beach," he explains, "[the 175th] Regiment had advanced 20km and eliminated the German corridor between the OMAHA and UTAH bridgeheads." The German "defensive system north of the Aure valley, from Isigny to Trevieres, collapsed," writes Reynolds. Perhaps most remarkable, opined Reynolds, was the fact that the 175th accomplished this feat of arms "on foot and with little or no sleep and food."[27] Historian Russell Weigley adds that the 175th's taking of Isigny snapped the left flank of the German 352nd Division, cutting it loose from the sea, dangling in the air.[28]

After taking Isigny, my father's regiment was ordered to move south toward Lison and la Fotelaie.[29] The regiment ran into stubborn resistance by German artillery and infantry, but took Lison and advanced to la Fotelaie by darkness on June 9.[30]

By June 10 and 11, 1944, the 29th Division as a whole was situated in proximity to the Vire and Elle Rivers, south of Isigny. On the 11th, according to the After Action Report, the division "spent the day consolidating positions [and] taking out pockets of resistance with patrols."[31]

The next day, as the 115th regiment moved "to secure St Claire-Sur-L'Elle-Couvains," the 175th was ordered to "mop up enemy resistance along Vire River, and maintain physical contact with 115th Inf on left."[32] That evening, two companies of my father's regiment crossed the Vire near Montmartin with orders to seize and hold bridges over a nearby canal. Tough enemy resistance, however, prevented those companies from getting past Montmartin. The remainder of the 175th consolidated its position.[33]

On June 13, 1944, the 175th engaged in tough and costly fighting near Montmartin, resulting in more than 200 casualties, including 53 killed. The next day, the 29th Division was transferred from V Corps (its corps since D-Day) to XIX Corps with orders to advance to the town of St. Lo, about 11 miles away.[34]

HEDGEROWS

The 29th Division was now in the *bocage* country of western France where for the next 35 days it engaged in one of the toughest battles of the Second World War: the Battle of the Hedgerows. For attacking infantry soldiers like my father, the hedgerows were a nightmare. Every hundred yards or so, fields were bounded by what my father later described as "high earthen walls, topped with brush, trees, and briar."[35] The Historical division of the War Department in an analysis of the St. Lo campaign written in 1946 described it as a "thankless, miserable, disheartening battle."[36] The nature of the fighting was perhaps best captured by Glover S. Johns, a battalion commander with the 29th Division's 115th infantry regiment, in his book, *The Clay Pigeons of St Lo.*

Johns described a seemingly endless series of little engagements where the American infantry measured success a yard at a time. German troops took full advantage of the natural fortresses created by the hedgerows, making the 29th Division fight and bleed for very small gains in territory. Behind each hedgerow was, potentially, German riflemen, machine guns, artillery pieces or mortars. The soldiers of the blue and gray division literally survived from hedgerow to hedgerow. "Thus goes the battle," noted Johns, "a rush, a pause, some creeping, a few isolated shots, some artillery fire, some mortars, some smoke, more creeping, another pause, dead silence, more firing, a great concentration of fire followed by a concerted rush. Then the whole process starts over again."[37]

The nature of the terrain so dominated the battlefield during this phase of the Normandy campaign that it is important to cite the many descriptions of the nature and impact of the hedgerows on the fighting.

Leo Daugherty, in his fine book *The Battle of the Hedgerows*, describes the battlefield as "a maze of broken and uneven terrain features surrounded by small plots of land enclosed by thick hedgerows that the French called *bocage*." The hedgerows, he writes, were "half-earthen embankments made up of both hedges and packed earth varying in thickness . . . and in heights." Small trees, bushes, and vines grew out of the hedgerows, explained Daugherty, and these "impeded both vision and movement."[38] Infantry squads, he wrote, slugged it out "from hedgerow to hedgerow."[39] For the German defenders, "each hedgerow was a potential fortress."[40]

Joseph Ewing described the 29th Division's approach to St. Lo as confronting "a vast maze of natural fortifications miles in depth." "Every hedgerow," he wrote, "was a possible enemy position," and the Germans "employed the hedgerows to the limit of their defensive capabilities and resisted bitterly."[41]

"Bocage," historian John Keegan writes, "for all the soldiers of the Liberation armies, . . . came to mean the sudden, unheralded burst of machine-pistol fire at close quarters, the crash and flame of a *panzerfaust* strike . . . ."[42]

Joseph Balkoski notes that the Germans, "nearly invisible in the *bocage*, contested almost every hedgerow." [43] "Whenever the 29ers stormed and won a hedgerow," he explained, "there always seemed to be another one 100 yards behind it resolutely defended by the enemy."[44] The Germans, from behind the hedgerows, fired machine guns, rifles, grenades, and mortars at the Americans. The soldiers of the 29th Division "were paying a demoralizing price for every foot of ground they gained."[45]

John C. McManus writes of the *bocage* that the Germans "could not have asked for terrain better suited to their objective of stalemating the Allies."[46]

The War Department's 1946 study of the St. Lo campaign described the battlefield as a "belt, six to ten miles deep, in which every feature of the terrain favored the German defense."[47] The two sides often fought fifty to one hundred yards apart and the fighting "came down to a matter of artillery bludgeoning and the infantry pushing through an endless series of defended fields and orchards."[48]

My father and the other men in his division dodged and ducked bullets, grenades, and shells in the hedgerows, advanced, if at all, cautiously from hedgerow to hedgerow, never knowing which one was defended by the Germans and never knowing how many Germans were present and what kind of weapons they had. "Each patch of farmland," writes James Jay Carafano, "became its own universe of battle."[49] This battle environment, noted one general officer, created feelings of "deadly unrelenting fatigue and danger."[50] General Omar Bradley called it, simply, the "Damndest country I've seen."[51]

This was the battlefield that my father entered on June 13, 1944. That same day, from the *bocage*, he wrote his first letters from "Somewhere in France."

"Dear Mom and Dad: Everything with me is fine . . . Plenty of excitement but will have to write about that later . . . Needless to say I'm busy . . . My home over here is a foxhole but rather comfortable . . . don't worry about me . . . Love Frankie."

He also wrote that day to his brother John. "Bet you're not surprised to hear that I'm now inside the Fortress of Europe," he exclaimed. "Am writing you this from my foxhole. That's now my home and rather comfortable at that considering everything . . . ." He told his brother that he has "had plenty of experiences to date but they will have to wait until later," explaining that he "[c]an't write too much as censorship will not permit it until a later date."

The next day, June 14, 1944, he noted in a letter to his parents that he wrote his first letter to them from France yesterday and that telling them about his "experiences" will have to come later.

The "experiences" that my father referenced in those first letters were, of course, landing on Omaha Beach on D-Day +1 under intermittent sniper and artillery fire; fighting at St Germaine-du Pert; capturing Isigny; and moving into the *bocage*.

The 29th Division's attack toward St. Lo began on June 16, 1944. It was led by the 175th regiment which attacked from south of the Elle River. My father's battalion made the most progress that day against scattered resistance and secured an area near the village of Amy.[52]

The next day, my father's battalion seized La Meauffe, about four miles from St. Lo.[53] On June 18, the 175th attacked toward La Creterie. [54] That same day, the 175th's 1st battalion engaged in a vicious fight for Hill 108 near Villiers-Fossard, and suffered 250 casualties, including 60 dead.[55]

On June 19, my father's battalion moved, in the face of heavy German mortar fire, to relieve the 1st battalion on Hill 108. The men of the 175th thereafter referred to this place as "Purple Heart Hill."[56]

"Plenty of experiences," my father wrote to his parents on June 18, "but as yet unable to write about them." He hinted, however, at the hard nature of the fighting in the *bocage*. "Whoever said 'war is hell,'" he wrote, "was right."

In letters written on June 19, my father lamented that he had not had the opportunity to bathe or change clothes in a while. He also wrote, "If I told you some of my experiences you'd probably worry so I just won't. However, it isn't a picnic by any chance."

The 29th Division's After Action Report notes that on June 19, 1944, "all three regiments remained in motion, conducting vigorous patrolling to the front and ranks."[57] The next day, my father's regiment and the 116th continued to patrol while the 115th attacked at Villiers-Fossard.[58]

On June 21, my father wrote to his parents that he needed a change of clothes but could not get one because his clothes "were on a jeep captured by the Germans." "Experiences galore in this war!," he noted.

General Bradley at this time ordered the 29th Division to temporarily cease attacking and revert to active defense on its front. This lasted until July 11. "Foxholes got deeper, fields of fire were cleared, barbed wire was strung," noted Joseph Ewing. But the enemy was still only a hedgerow away, and artillery and mortar fire continued to pose a constant danger.[59]

Each battalion in the division took turns getting a brief period of rest behind the front lines.[60] My father informed his parents in a June 22nd letter that he was enjoying "the first opportunity . . . to get some sleep in quite some time." He noted further that he received their package containing cookies, peanuts, and candy, and mentioned that he was planning to have "some of your cookies and try to take a nap of a few hours."

Two days later, he assured his parents that he was okay. "For heaven's sake don't worry so much," he wrote. "It's not going to do you any good."

On June 30, my father wrote that he was having "plenty of experiences," but would not be able to tell about them "until I get back."

The division's After Action Report for June 1944 concluded by noting that between June 6 and June 30, the division "had advanced about eighteen miles," and was "in constant contact with the enemy."[61]

There was plenty of hard fighting ahead. My father was still stuck in hedgerow country. St. Lo still had to be taken. The Germans were not giving ground easily. Exhaustion and fatigue were ever present among the troops. The 29th Division had been bloodied. Its three infantry regiments and support units suffered more than 4600 casualties, including 1,137 killed in June. The numbers for my father's regiment in June were 286 killed, 795 wounded, 50 injured, and 187 missing for a casualty total of 1,318 men.[62] And much more blood would have to be spilled to win the war.

During the first nine days of July 1944, the 29th Division, with a total manpower force of 14,290, continued to consolidate and strengthen its defensive positions on the front lines. Infantry regiments engaged in "active patrolling," and were involved in "several minor skirmishes."[63]

The division's After Action Report notes that during this time "a system was worked out to enable infantry reinforced with tanks to advance against the German hedgerow defenses."[64] The system involved attaching metal prongs to the fronts of tanks to poke holes in the hedgerows. Demolition charges would then be placed and detonated in the holes, blasting gaps for tanks to move through. The tanks would then fire their 75mm guns and machine guns at the next hedgerow, being followed closely by infantry.[65] This required close coordination between small groups of "infantry-tank-engineer teams." These tactics had been carefully rehearsed before used in the *bocage*.[66]

On July 1, 1944, my father reminded his parents that in five days he would be 28 years old. "Time sure does fly, doesn't it," he wrote.

The next day, Supreme Allied Commander General Dwight Eisenhower and Commander of the 1st U.S. Army General Omar Bradley visited the 29th Division's headquarters near St. Claire-sur-Elle.[67]

In a letter written on July 3, my father noted that, "It's July 4th tomorrow are they having fireworks back in the states? Here we have them everyday." The next day, he informed his parents that he was "awarded an Expert Infantry Badge," and noted that it meant an additional $5 per month in pay. He referred to his upcoming birthday and remarked that he was "[g]etting rather international spending consecutive birthdays in the U.S.A., England and France." "Maybe," he continued, "my next one will be spent in the good old U.S.A."

In a July 6 letter, he wrote that he was "enjoying a day of rest" on his birthday. He was writing the letter, he noted, from a USO Club and mentioned that he had a bath and a change of clothes. In a second letter written that day, he mentioned visiting a Red Cross club, too.

Three days later, however, he wrote that he was back in his foxhole. The rest period was coming to an end.

The After Action Report notes that on July 10, the 175th regiment "was relieved of its defensive positions by the 35th Inf Div, and moved to an assembly area in Div res[erve], vicinity St. Claire-sur-Elle."[68]

That assembly area was the jump off point for my father's regiment's participation in the culminating eight-day attack to capture St. Lo. The final push would be plagued by rain, fog, mud, uncoordinated attacks, and the ever present hedgerows.

ST. LO

The 29th Division was joined by the 30th and 35th Divisions in the final push to take St. Lo. The 29th's attack began on July 11, with elements of the division jumping off from across an eight-mile front from la Meauffe to Villiers-Fossard to the Couvains-Calvaire road.[69] The immediate targets of the initial assault were German positions on the Martinville Ridge. The 115th, 116th, and one battalion of the 175th attacked with elements of the 35th Division. Initially, the 175th's other two battalions, including my father's, were in reserve poised to exploit any opportunities created by the initial assaults. That day, my father wrote to his parents that he couldn't sleep the previous night because of enemy artillery. "Twas a bit noisy," he wrote.

The next day, my father's battalion was ordered to join the attack on Martinville Ridge. That day, wrote Joseph Balkoski, Martinville Ridge "was a shooting gallery . . . ."[70] My father's battalion, after moving forward only 300 yards, ran into artillery, mortar, and small arms fire.[71] In this brief forward movement, the 175th's 2nd and 3rd battalions suffered nearly 60 casualties.[72] The 29th Division as a whole suffered 489 casualties on July 12.[73]

On July 13, my father's regiment was ordered to attack through the 116th regiment near la Boulaye. The 175th attacked at 8:00am, and met "heavy small arms fire and intense . . . artillery and mortar fire."[74] The After Action Report notes that the 175th "was unable to advance any appreciable distance."[75] John McManus explains that the 175th's attack stalled almost immediately because its "communications were out" and it had "little tank support."[76] Also, McManus noted, the 175th's 3rd battalion "ran into a wall of fire," and "casualties were heavy."[77]

My father mentioned in a letter dated July 13 that it had been raining for a few days and noted that "this fighting . . . doesn't give one very much time off." He also wrote that, "We are giving the Jerries a damn good beating . . . ."

The next day, my father wrote to his parents that he had twice attempted to write to them but "[e]verytime I start the shells start thick and fast and I have to give up." He told them that he has been "busy as the dickens so far today. Hope it lets up a bit this afternoon." He concluded the letter by noting that he was "a bit tired after being in the front lines for almost 40 days. Hope we soon get some rest."

In another letter that day, my father wrote: "Really am tired today. The last few days have been tough. In fact having been in the front lines for almost 40 days is no picnic. Hope there is a rest in site."

In hindsight, these letters manifest the fatigue and near exhaustion caused by weeks of hedgerow fighting.

On July 16, my father noted in a letter that he had received in the mail copies of the *Scranton Tribune* "telling all about the [Normandy] invasion." He then remarked that, "Being in it and reading all about it gives one a very different feeling." He also mentioned that he slept a little bit last night "although the shells were rather thick for awhile."

On July 17, my father told his parents that if they could see him now they would probably faint. "Never have I been as dirty and needed a change of clothing . . . ." He also noted that he "was being kept . . . busy."

That day, the 29th Division began its final assault on St. Lo. All regiments attacked toward the objective. The 175th attacked southwest along the St. Lo-Bayeaux highway.[78] In two letters written during this period, my father hinted at the grueling nature of the fighting approaching St. Lo. "Can't find much to write about that would interest you," he told his parents. "War is hell so why talk about it." A day after St. Lo fell to the 29th and other American divisions, my father wrote that he had "[j]ust been reading Esquire magazine about how some people have been abusing the servicemen coming home from the fronts." He angrily suggested that "they should send those people over here to see what it is like."

A task force of the 29th Division and support units entered St. Lo on July 18, 1944. "The Americans could hardly believe the destruction before their eyes," writes John McManus. "The roofs of houses were caved in, the streets were choked with rubble, telephone poles were down, trees were scattered everywhere, and masonry was heaped in ugly piles all over the place."[79] St. Lo, writes Michael Reynolds, "was a wasteland of rubble with almost no undamaged buildings and hardly any distinguishable roads."[80] St. Lo, like so many towns and cities in the Second World War, was nearly destroyed before it was liberated. As they retreated from the town, German forces shelled the Americans with artillery and mortars, causing further casualties and destruction.

On July 20, the 29th Division was relieved by the 35th Division and moved back to the area behind the lines near St. Claire-sur-Elle.[81]

The Battle of the Hedgerows cost the 29th Division 3,706 casualties, and similar numbers for the 30th and 35th Divisions. Thus, American forces suffered nearly 11,000 casualties to advance four-to-seven miles along the front and capture St. Lo.[82] It was the costliest campaign in the 29th Division's history.

The tough, grueling fight for this part of Normandy was not foreseen by Allied war planners. The invasion forces did not receive training in England to fight in hedgerows. Tactics to advance through this countryside were devised and adapted during the fight. The rainy, foggy weather limited the effective use of air power to support the infantry. The terrain--rain soaked fields bounded by the ubiquitous hedgerows--limited the effectiveness of tanks and forced the infantry to make slow, costly advances measured in yards instead of miles. In an interview published in the *Scranton Tribune* on July 8, 1945, after he returned home from overseas, my father noted about the fight for St. Lo that "The going was tough there until . . . bombers in wave after wave all flying low pulverized the enemy position."[83]

Nevertheless, British historian Max Hastings calls the American campaign to capture St. Lo "one of First Army's outstanding feats of arms . . . ." It set the stage, explained Hastings, "for the supreme American military achievement of the Normandy campaign, Operation COBRA."[84]

After spending 43 days on the front lines, participating in some of the most brutal combat of the Second World War, my father and his division enjoyed a nine-day rest period.

During that rest period, my father and other battle-hardened soldiers were able to get haircuts, shaves, take a bath or shower, watch movies and USO shows, listen to war news on the radio, and write letters home.[85] On July 22, my father told his parents that he was "getting a little rest, for how long I don't know." The next day he noted that he was "getting ready to go to church services" and was "still enjoying a bit of a rest . . . ." On July 24, he wrote that he had "just returned from an afternoon show: Spencer Tracy in 'A Guy Named Joe.'" On July 25, he wrote that he was attempting to locate some "boys from Avoca." "Still resting a bit," he noted, "but don't know how much longer it will continue." On July 27, he wrote that he was enjoying the rest, but noted that it came "after days of continuous action."

The division's rest period also included additional training, absorbing new replacements, and the dedication of an American cemetery at la Cambe. A plaque at the cemetery read: "June 1944 by the 29th Infantry Division, . . . as a final resting place for officers and men of that division who made the supreme sacrifice on the battlefield of Normandy." "We who carry on the fight," the inscription continued, "salute these comrades, and other honored dead of the division who could not be buried here." There was a roll call of the dead, and taps were sounded.[86]

My father's division moved back to the front lines beginning on July 28. The 175th regiment led the way to an assembly area near la Denisiere. The men were subjected to small arms fire and shelling along the way, and German planes dropped anti-personnel bombs at night.[87]

On July 30, my father's regiment ran into tough enemy resistance by infantry and tanks. The 175th's headquarters was shelled intensively by German artillery.

On August 1, "all units of the Division resumed the attack."[88] The 175th was ordered to seize and secure high ground just north of the Villebaudon-Tessy-sur-Vire Road.[89] That day, my father wrote to his brother John that it was "pretty rugged over here," and noted that he was "still in the thick of things." He was anxious, he wrote, "to get this mess over real soon so that we might get back home." He also wrote to his parents that day. "Things here aren't too bad," he told them. "Who knows but that it won't be very much longer until this mess is over."

On August 2, the division's attack toward the town of Vire continued, with my father's regiment in position to support the advance of the 115th and 116th regiments.[90] My father wrote in a letter that day that "all goes well with me thus far. Hope my luck holds out as it won't be long before this mess is over."

For the next two weeks, the 29th Division moved against stiff resistance to capture Vire and the high ground to its south. Vire, like St. Lo, had been pounded by American bombers and long-range artillery since D-Day, but the destruction intensified after the capture of St. Lo.

Vire, a town of about 8,000 inhabitants located near the Vire River, was "an old fortress town whose history dated back to medieval times."[91] The town was defended by German infantry and paratroopers armed with mines, anti-tank guns, artillery, and mortars. "The fighting," writes John McManus, "was similar to what had transpired in July--coordinated bloody assaults, hedgerow to hedgerow, against resolute defenders who often fought to the death."[92]

On August 4, my father wrote an optimistic letter to his parents. "War news is very encouraging," he noted, "and optimists, and even others, say it won't be long now. Here's hoping it isn't. Personally, I've had my share of this war . . . ."

The next day, he told his parents that he had spent a few days in a hospital with a "minor stomach ailment." He also wrote that the French people were "thus far hard to understand. A good portion [of them] border on indifference." He also noted, however, that he had "been too busy on the front and haven't gotten into towns so I don't know what they have to offer there if anything."

One week later, August 12, 1944, my father, in the wake of the tough fight for Vire, wrote that he was "[f]eeling very tired today. Was up all night and all morning." "Foremost thought in all our minds," he continued, is "when are we going to get any rest. Surely it must come to that soon . . . Someday when this is all over I'll write a book." He noted further that except for a short time period, "we've been in this thing since it started." "The going," he wrote, "is tough."

In mid-August, after the capture of Vire, the exhausted men of the 29th Division took a brief rest in rear area camps to prepare for a renewal of the offensive. All units received new clothing, and the men were able to bathe, watch movies and USO shows, receive packages and write letters home. They also trained, especially the replacement troops.[93]

The war news, with Paris soon to be liberated and German troops being pushed further east, raised expectations among the 29th Division soldiers that the end of the war might be in sight. "Not a single 29er," writes Joseph Balkoski, "could harbor any doubt that his side was going to win the war--and soon."[94] Joseph Ewing noted that "[h]ighly encouraging war bulletins tended . . . to bolster the morale of the 29th Division veteran . . . The thrill of victory . . . had taken possession of the troops."[95]

On August 17, my father wrote to his parents that he sent home some souvenirs, including a bayonet, canteen, German helmet, gas mask carrier, and a shoulder strap "formerly worn by Hitler's No. 1 troops. At least they were his No. 1. Now they're not even rated." He also mentioned that he was going to a show that night, showered in the morning, and slept well last night. My father also mentioned that he heard from his brother Eddie. "I guess I'll be seeing him over here soon," he wrote. "I'll be looking for him." The next day, he noted that he enjoyed a shower and a change of clothes.

It is clear from my father's letters that in war, many simple things we take for granted become luxuries. A bath, a change of clothes, a shave, watching a movie or show, receiving mail and packages from home are all noteworthy events.

On August 19, my father told his parents that his brother Eddie was in England. He also noted that he had planned to see Dinah Shore at a USO show, but didn't because it rained.

The next day, still enjoying the rest period, my father wrote that it was a beautiful Sunday in France and mentioned that he "attended church in a nearby village." "War news," he wrote, "is bright and there is no telling when the end will come. My guess is it will end abruptly."

On August 24, my father wrote that he was "taking it easy today." "War news gets better with each passing day," he noted. "Maybe we'll be home for X-mas."

The division's After Action Report notes that on August 22 and 23, the men "conducted training in the assault of fortified positions," street fighting and the use of "scaling ladders, flame throwers, and pole charges." The next two days, the report notes, were used to move the division to the assembly area in preparation for attack.[96]

BREST

On August 25, 1944, Allied forces liberated Paris. That day, at approximately 1:00pm, the 29th Division began its attack toward the French port of Brest on the Brittany peninsula.

France's Brittany peninsula juts out into the Atlantic Ocean, "pointing like an extended index finger toward the New World."[97] The port of Brest, France's second largest port in 1944, is located near the far western tip of the peninsula. Brest was used to disembark U.S. troops and equipment of the American Expeditionary Force during the First World War. Its significance as a target for Allied forces in the Second World War derived from the importance of logistics. As the American invading forces established a beachhead after D-Day, more and more troops would be needed to overcome German resistance throughout France and, ultimately, Germany. The more secure ports in allied possession, the greater the ability to pour more troops into the fight and supply them with the needed fuel and equipment.

In the spring and summer of 1944, Brest was a city of about 100,000 people. The occupied city was defended by 40,000 to 50,000 German troops commanded by General Hermann-Bernhard Ramcke, a 35-year veteran of the *Wehrmacht* who had served in all three branches of the German armed forces.

The Germans had constructed U-boat pens at Brest, and Hitler had ordered the city held to the last man.

Joseph Ewing described the defenses of Brest as "an abundance of strong-points . . . forming a great defensive arc that swept around the city," and an "inner band of ramparts . . . with steel pillboxes, anti-tank ditches, road barriers, and minefields."[98] The topography around Brest also favored the defenders, with ridges, hills, and deep valleys crossed by several streams. [99]

U.S. armored columns had swept through the Brittany peninsula in early August, reaching the outer environs of Brest, but were ultimately ordered to abandon the effort to take Brest, leaving a small force to contain the German forces in the city.[100] It would take infantry in large numbers to capture Brest.

The decision to take Brest has been mired in controversy since the end of the war. Critics of the effort have argued that it was a costly and unnecessary campaign that drew significant resources away from the post-Normandy breakout toward the east designed to thrust into the Siegfried Line. Historian Russell Weigley is typical of the many critics, arguing that both Eisenhower and Bradley were too wedded to the original Overlord plan even when events rendered the taking of Brest unnecessary. The Americans' excessive caution and inflexible leadership, Weigley and others contend, prevented them from adjusting their plans and seizing the greater opportunity in the east.

Another historian is quoted as labeling the infantry attack on Brest as a "huge military embarrassment," and accusing Bradley of a "failure of generalship" in refusing to adjust outdated plans.[101]

In his autobiography, *A General's Life*, Bradley defended his decision to take Brest on two main grounds. First, Brest was thought at the time to be essential to American logistics for the northwest Europe campaign. "[L]ogistics," explained Bradley, "were the lifeblood of the Allied armies in France. Without ports and facilities we could not supply our armies."[102] When Bradley ordered Brest taken, the U.S. still had use of only a single French port: Cherbourg.[103] Brest and the other Brittany ports, Bradley explained, would enable us to get more supplies, including food, ammunition, weapons, equipment, and fuel, to the troops in the field.

Second, according to Bradley, it would have been "militarily imprudent" to leave Ramcke and his large garrison at Brest intact to potentially harass our forces from the rear.[104]

British Prime Minister Winston Churchill, in the final volume of his history of the Second World War, weighed in on Bradley's side of the argument. "Brest," he wrote, "which held a large garrison, under an active commander, was dangerous, and had to be eliminated."[105]

At least two recent historians of the Brest campaign also side with Bradley in this controversy. Jonathan Gawne, in his *1944, Americans in Brittany: The Battle for Brest*, concludes that the effort to seize Brest "was . . . probably the right thing to do at the time--given all the information available to the commanders in the field."[106] Joseph Balkoski concurs, opining that the American commanders' judgment about taking Brest "reflected the shifting strategic situation and demonstrated a realistic and flexible plan of action that any far- sighted commander would have followed."[107]

Whatever the ultimate verdict of history on the wisdom of the Brest campaign, nothing can detract from the hard fighting, sacrifice, and bravery of the American soldiers, including the men of the 29th Division, who fought and, in some cases, died there.

The Brest offensive included soldiers from the 29th, 8th, and 2nd Infantry Divisions. The 29th Division, traveling from the south of Vire on August 22, arrived near Brest after a 36-hour, 200-mile motorized trip through such towns as St. James, Medreac, Plougernevel, and Huelgoat. The French populations of these towns and villages greeted the 29th's soldiers as heroes and liberators.[108] Each regiment of the division had its own truck, trailer, and jeep convoys to move troops, equipment, and supplies. It was an enormous logistical effort to get an entire division and its supply requirements from Vire to near Brest in a short time period. The division's convoys stretched some 40 miles in length.[109]

As the 29th division troops motored west toward Brest, General George S. Patton's Third Army, as part of operation COBRA, raced in the opposite direction toward the Seine River and, ultimately, the Siegfried Line. I recall my father telling me about the remarkable speed of the trucks and tanks in Patton's army as they moved east during that time. "It seemed," he said, "as if the trucks' tires were off the ground, they were going so fast."

The 29th Division's attack began on August 25. The combat veterans of the division, like my father, soon learned that the terrain near Brest combined with the well-prepared German defenses "produced the same slow, dusty and bloody fighting as the division had experienced before."[110]

My father's regiment, after being assigned to guard the right flank of the division's other two regiments on August 25, moved near Plouzane on August 26 and attacked Hill 103, which was considered to be the key to the city of Brest.[111] In American hands, Hill 103 would overlook the western and northwestern approaches to Brest.[112]

During the next several days, the struggle to take Hill 103 "would go down in the history of the 175th Infantry as one of the toughest battles of World War II."[113]

The initial task of seizing the hill fell to the 175th's 1st battalion, which made early progress, but soon ran into small arms, artillery, and machine gun fire that stopped the advance.[114]

As the struggle continued and intensified, the regiment's other two battalions, including my father's, were committed to the attack. The division's After Action Report for September 1944 describes the enemy's resistance on Hill 103 as "determined" and "extremely heavy," noting the "intense artillery fire" of the German defenders.[115]

Hill 103 had been fortified, writes Balkoski, "with a diligence reminiscent of the trench lines and redoubts on the Western Front in World War I."[116] The German defenses included dugouts, trenches, stone pillboxes, caves, tunnels, mines, and barbed wire. The 175th's intelligence officer remarked that "Enemy positions were well dug in, cleverly concealed, and [their occupants] resisted our advance with typical paratroop fanaticism."[117]

Over the course of three days, my father's regiment inched its way up the hill, and by August 29 the Germans were nearly surrounded. The commander of the 175th, Colonel William Purnell, ordered an unusual and costly night attack, which enabled the 175th to take the hill. The regiment suffered nearly 200 casualties in the struggle to seize Hill 103, and still had to defend it against German artillery attacks.[118] The division as a whole suffered 1200 casualties in only seven days of fighting.

After securing Hill 103, the division consolidated its position and prepared to advance to the city. The position on Hill 103 "gave the 29th a marvelous view of the city of Brest."[119] It overlooked Forts Keranroux and Montbarry and what came to be known as "Sugarloaf Hill," all German strongpoints.

On September 6, the XIX Tactical Air Command flew 18 sorties, dropping more than 100 tons of bombs and strafing enemy positions.[120] This enabled all three regiments of the 29th to advance. The next day, all regiments probed enemy positions in an effort to discern new enemy strongpoints.[121]

From September 8 to 18, the 29th Division engaged in combat actions every day in its advance toward Brest. The 175th, my father's regiment, battled for control of Fort Keranoux. It was during the approach to Keranoux near Ilioc farm that a sergeant in the 175th, Sherwood Hallman, of Spring City, Pennsylvania, earned the Congressional Medal of Honor for single-handedly leaping into a central area of German defenses, wounding four enemy soldiers and capturing 87 others, thereby enabling his battalion to advance 2000 yards. The Medal was awarded posthumously because Sgt. Hallman was killed by enemy fire the following day.[122]

Joseph Balkoski notes that by the time they reached Ilioc, my father's regiment "had fought nothing but brutal toe-to-toe slugfests for two weeks against an implacable enemy from Plouzane to Hill 103 to Ilioc," suffering about 700 casualties. "Here," he writes, "was war at its most gruesome."[123] And after Ilioc, the 175th would move to take Keranoux and a mound of earth dubbed "Sugarloaf Hill."

Fort Keranoux, a 19th century fortress, was surrounded by anti-tank ditches and dug-in positions connected by trenches. German defenders had automatic weapons, anti-aircraft guns, and 88mm cannon at every approach to the fort.[124] Keranoux was pounded by artillery for about two hours, creating deep shell craters, then stormed by the 175th, and seized rather quickly. The After Action Report states that with the 2nd battalion leading the way "[i]n just 20 minutes the capture was complete."[125] The 175th suffered only 10 casualties and captured more than 100 German prisoners.[126]

Sugarloaf Hill, also called "Butts," was a mound of earth originally built by the French that the Germans had converted to a fortress, with concrete gun emplacements and tunnels. The 1st battalion of the 175th attacked, seized and neutralized Sugarloaf Hill after two hours of tough fighting.[127] My father's battalion, meanwhile, maintained the defense of the recently captured Fort Keranoux.[128]

Southwest from Fort Keranoux, the 29th Division's 115th and 116th regiments battled for four days to overcome heavy German resistance to seize Fort Montbarry. By September 16, all regiments of the 29th Division were on the outskirts of Brest. The capture of the city was only two days away.

On September 5, in the aftermath of the struggle for Hill 103, and in the midst of the approach to Brest, my father wrote to his parents that "Everything goes well so far." He noted, however, that "the going is tough, but we are tougher. . ." He also wrote that the "war news is very good," and suggested that he might be "walking in" on his parents in the near future.

Five days later, my father noted to his parents that he had "been busy all day." "Everything with me," he assured his parents, "is ok despite the tough sledding."

On September 11, he explained in a letter to his parents that *Stars and Stripes* magazine "carried the new demobilization plan to become effective when Germany falls . . . Its to be based on a point system taking in years of service, no. of months overseas, time in combat, dependency, etc." He continued, "Guess we will have to wait until Germany falls to see how it works out."

The next day, he mentioned in a letter that he was "still in the thick of things." "I'm a bit tired," he wrote. "Had a busy day and probably a busy night ahead."

On September 13, as the struggle for the forts continued for the 175th, my father wrote that he was "still in the thick of things. So far all goes well. Hope it keeps up that way."

Three days later, he again wrote that he was "still in the thick of things," but assured his parents that "so far all goes well."

The description of the fighting near Brest by the After Action Reports and the historians of the 29th Division gives more meaning to what my father meant when he wrote that he was "still in the thick of things," or was "busy," or noted that the "going was tough." The fights for Hill 103, Forts Keranoux and Montbarry, and Sugarloaf Hill were deadly struggles that produced many casualties. On September 13 alone, my father's regiment lost 90 men and the 115th lost 71 men.[129]

On September 16, 1944, my father's battalion mopped up enemy resistance near Sugarloaf Hill and reached the city wall of Brest.[130]

The stage was set for the final American assault on Brest by the 29th, 2nd, and 8th infantry divisions and their support units. All three regiments of the 29th Division participated in the final attack, with the 116th in the center, the 115th on the right, and the 175th (my father's) on the left.

My father's regiment attacked toward the old city wall, and became the first troops to enter the city.[131] The battle-hardened troops engaged in urban warfare, clearing rubble-strewn streets and buildings. Assisting the infantry were flame-throwing tanks called "Crocodiles." Enemy snipers were all around the city.

By nightfall on September 17, the 175th had fought to the banks of the Penfeld River, inflicting many casualties and capturing more than 600 enemy prisoners.[132] On September 18, American forces of all three infantry divisions "fanned out into the maze of rubble-strewn streets and headed for the harborside."[133] Troops entered the massive submarine pens, and some gathered souvenirs.

The German surrender of the city came in separate episodes. One group of German soldiers surrendered to the 29th Division. Another group surrendered to the 2nd Division. Almost 10,000 prisoners were taken. The soldiers of the 29th, writes Balkoski, "watched thousands of bedraggled and compliant enemy soldiers, sailors, and airmen materialize . . . from their hiding places with their hands up."[134] On September 19 and 20, additional enemy forces surrendered to the 8th Division.

The fight to seize Brest cost the Americans more than 9800 casualties. The 29th Division suffered more than 2300 casualties, including more than 320 killed.[135]

On September 19, my father wrote in a letter that "it . . . has been a busy day for me. Have been on the go since early morning." Two days later, my father noted that while the war news was good, and he would like to get home for Christmas, "I'm afraid it will be longer than that."

It would indeed be longer than that, because after taking Brest and being given a short rest, the 29th Division was ordered by General Bradley to return to the 1st Army, move by train and truck convoy to southern Holland, and prepare for entering Germany. The final phase of my father's journey through the Second World War was about to begin.

Meanwhile, Brest was in ruins. It was, writes Martin Blumenson, a "totally destroyed city and a thoroughly demolished port." "The desolation," he wrote, "was appalling." This was a result of Allied bombing and shelling and German sabotage. The Penfeld River channel was blocked by damaged bridge structures. "The wharves, drydocks, cranes along the waterfront, even the breakwaters enclosing the naval basin and the commercial port, had been ruined," notes Blumenson. The harbor was littered with scuttled ships.[136]

As noted previously, the Overlord plan called for seizing Brest and other Atlantic and Channel ports to logistically facilitate the exploitation of the Normandy beachhead and the breakout from Normandy. Brest, it was hoped, would be able to be used to accept troops and equipment directly from the United States to supplement the troops arriving from England. General Eisenhower had prudently planned for all circumstances, including the possibility that Channel ports would not be captured for sometime after the Normandy invasion.

Critics of the Brest campaign, with the benefit of hindsight, call it unnecessary and a tragic waste of American lives for little or no benefit. They further claim that it diverted important resources from the race across France and thereby contributed to lengthening the war.

In war, the unexpected happens, interfering with the most meticulous and well crafted plans. None of the Overlord planners and decision-makers could predict which ports would fall and when. Nor could they have foreseen that when Brest did fall, it would be in such a state of disrepair as to be unusable as a significant logistical port of entry for more troops and supplies. Furthermore, the Overlord planners could not predict with any certainty the pace and distance of the breakout from the beachhead by Allied forces. By the time Brest was securely in-American control, Paris had been liberated and allied forces were racing toward the Siegfried Line.

These questions of grand strategy, of course, were not on the minds of the men of the 29th Division, including my father. They were given a task to perform and they did it. Like they had been doing since Omaha Beach, American infantrymen were slugging it out with a determined enemy, gaining ground slowly but inexorably. Cities and towns were liberated, prisoners were captured, and many brave soldiers died or suffered wounds in the effort.

The Battle for Brest rarely receives recognition by World War II historians and commentators. It is in some sense a forgotten battle of the Second World War. Perhaps *Yank Magazine* explained it best in 1944, shortly after the battle: "The siege of Brest probably will never receive the world-wide recognition it rightfully deserves . . . [I]t [was] one of the hardest battles fought by American infantry in Europe since 1918." The men who fought it, surely, deserve that recognition.

NOTES

1. Balkoski, *Beyond the Beachhead*, p. 147.
2. Quoted in Reynolds, *Eagles and Bulldogs*, p. 97.
3. Reynolds, *Eagles and Bulldogs*, pp. 56-57.
4. John C. McManus, *The Americans at Normandy: The Summer of 1944--The American War from the Normandy Beaches to Falaise* (New York: Tom Doherty Associates, L.L.C. 2004), p. 18.
5. Balkoski, *Beyond the Beachhead*, p. 146.
6. Glover S. Johns, *The Clay Pigeons of St. Lo* (Mechanicsville, PA: Stackpole Books 2002), p. 253.
7. Reynolds, *Eagles and Bulldogs*, p. 119.
8. Balkoski, *Beyond the Beachhead*, p. 152.
9. McManus, *The Americans at Normandy*, p. 36.
10. Ewing, *29 Let's Go*, p. 62.
11. Balkoski, *Beyond the Beachhead*, p. 152.
12. Frank F. Sempa, *Scranton Tribune* (June 6, 1969).
13. Balkoski, *Beyond the Beachhead*, p. 154.
14. *After Action Report*, 29th division, 175th Infantry, June 1944; www.29infantrydivision.org/WWII%20Documents
15. *After Action Report*, 29th Division, June 1944.
16. *After Action Report*, 29th Division, 175th Infantry, June 1944.
17. Ewing, *29 Let's Go*, p. 63.
18. Reynolds, *Eagles and Bulldogs*, p. 121.
19. Reynolds, *Eagles and Bulldogs*, p. 121.
20. Ewing, *29 Let's Go*, p. 63.

21. *After Action Report*, 29th Division, 175th Infantry, June 1944; Reynolds, *Eagles and Bulldogs*, p. 123.

22. *After Action Report*, 29th Division, 175th Infantry, June 1944; Ewing, *29 Let's Go*, p. 63.

23. McManus, *The Americans at Normandy*, p. 40.

24. McManus, *The Americans at Normandy*, p. 40.

25. Ewing, *29 Let's Go*, p. 63.

26. *After Action Report*, 29th Division, June 1944.

27. Reynolds, *Eagles and Bulldogs*, p. 124.

28. Russell F. Weigley, *Eisenhower's Lieutenants: The Campaigns of France and Germany, 1944-1945* (Bloomington, Ind: Indiana University Press 1981), p. 143.

29. *After Action Report*, 29th Division, 175th Infantry, June 1944.

30. Ewing, *29 Let's Go*, p. 64-66.

31. *After Action Report*, 29th Division, June 1944.

32. *After Action Report*, 29th Division, June 1944.

33. *After Action Report*, 29th Division, June 1944.

34. Ewing, *29 Let's Go*, p. 83.

35. Sempa, *Scranton Tribune*, June 6, 1969.

36. David Garth and Charles H. Taylor, *St-Lo* (Washington D.C.: War Department 1946), p. 125.

37. Quoted in Stephen E. Ambrose, *Citizen Soldiers: The U.S. Army From the Normandy Beaches to the Bulge to the Surrender of Germany* (New York: Touchstone 1997), p. 61-62.

38. Leo Daugherty, *The Battle of the Hedgerows: Bradley's First Army in Normandy, June-July 1944* (London: Brown Partworks Limited 2001), p. 15.

39. Daugherty, *Battle of the Hedgerows*, p. 9.

40. Daugherty, *Battle of the Hedgerows*, p. 45.

41. Ewing, *29 Let's Go*, p. 75.

42. John Keegan, *Six Armies in Normandy: From D-Day to the Liberation of Paris* (New York: Penguin Books 1982), p. 153.

43. Balkoski, *Beyond the Beachhead*, p. 212.

44. Balkoski, *Beyond the Beachhead*, p. 190.

45. Balkoski, *Beyond the Beachhead*, p. 212.

46. McManus, *The Americans at Normandy*, p. 177.

47. Garth and Taylor, *St-Lo*, p. 2.

48. Garth and Taylor, *St-Lo*, p. 125.

49. James Jay Carafano, *After D-Day: Operation Cobra and the Normandy Breakout* (Boulder, Colo: Lynne Rienner Publishers 2000), p. 27.

50. Quoted in Garth and Taylor, *St-Lo*, p. 125.

51. Weigley, *Eisenhower's Lieutenants*, p. 145.

52. *After Action Report*, 29th Division, June 1944; Reynolds, *Eagles and Bulldogs*, p. 40; Ewing, *29 Let's Go*, p. 84.

53. Balkoski, *Beyond the Beachhead*, p. 212-213.

54. *After Action Report*, 29th Division, June 1944.

55. Ewing, *29 Let's Go*, p. 85; Reynolds, *Eagles and Bulldogs*, p. 141.

56. Ewing, *29 Let's Go*, p. 87; Balkoski, *Beyond the Beachhead*, p. 215.
57. *After Action Report*, 29th Division, June 1944.
58. *After Action Report*, 29th Division, June 1944.
59. Ewing, *29 Let's Go*, p. 88.
60. Balkoski, *Beyond the Beachhead*, p. 229.
61. *After Action Report*, 29th Division, June 1944.
62. Ewing, *29 Let's Go*, p. 304.
63. *After Action Report*, 29th Division, July 1944.
64. *After Action Report*, 29th Division, July 1944.
65. Balkoski, *Beyond the Beachhead*, p. 231-232.
66. Garth and Taylor, *St-Lo*, p. 56.
67. Balkoski, *Beyond the Beachhead*, p. 233.
68. *After Action Report*, 29th Division, July 1944.
69. Daugherty, *Battle of the Hedgerows*, p. 168.
70. Balkoski, *Beyond the Beachhead*, p. 248.
71. *After Action Report*, 29th Division, July 1944.
72. Balkoski, *Beyond the Beachhead*, p. 248.
73. Reynolds, *Eagles and Bulldogs*, p. 182.
74. *After Action Report*, 29th Division, July 1944.
75. *After Action Report*, 29th Division, July 1944.
76. McManus, *Americans at Normandy*, p. 252.
77. McManus, *Americans at Normandy*, p. 252.
78. *After Action Report*, 29th Division, July 1944; Ewing, *29 Let's Go*, p. 97.
79. McManus, *Americans at Normandy*, p. 268-269.
80. Reynolds, *Eagles and Bulldogs*, p. 192-193.
81. Reynolds, *Eagles and Bulldogs*, p. 195.
82. Garth and Taylor, *St-Lo*, p. 126.
83. *Scranton Tribune*, July 8, 1945.
84. Max Hastings, *Overlord: D-Day & the Battle for Normandy* (New York: Simon & Schuster 1984), p. 249.
85. Ewing, *29 Let's Go*, p. 105.
86. Ewing, *29 Let's Go*, p. 105.
87. Ewing, *29 Let's Go*, p. 107-110.
88. *After Action Report*, 29th Division, August 1944.
89. *After Action Report*, 29th Division, august 1944.
90. *After Action Report*, 29th Division, August 1944.
91. McManus, *Americans at Normandy*, p. 357.
92. McManus, *Americans at Normandy*, p. 357.
93. *After Action Report*, 29th Division, August 1944.
94. Joseph Balkoski, *From Beachhead to Brittany: The 29th Infantry Division at Brest, August-September 1944* (Mechanicsburg, PA: Stackpole Books 2008), p. 2.
95. Ewing, *29 Let's Go*, p. 120.
96. *After Action Report*, 29th Division, August 1944.
97. Joseph Balkoski, *From Beachhead to Brittany*, p. 2.
98. Ewing, *29 Let's Go*, p. 121.

99. Weigley, *Eisenhower's Lieutenants*, p. 414.

100. Balkoski, *From Beachhead to Brittany*, p. 5-6.

101. Quoted in Balkoski, *From Beachhead to Brittany*, p. 7.

102. Omar Bradley, *A General's Life* (New York: Simon and Schuster 1983), p. 285.

103. Bradley, *A General's Life*, p. 286.

104. Bradley, *A General's Life*, p. 286.

105. Winston S. Churchill, *Triumph and Tragedy* (Boston: Houghton Mifflin Company 1953), p. 32.

106. Jonathan Gawne, *1944, Americans in Brittany: The Battle for Brest*, (Paris: Histore & Collections 2002), p. 158.

107. Balkoski, *From Beachhead to Brittany*, p. 342.

108. Balkoski, *From Beachhead to Brittany*, p. 11, 15.

109. Balkoski, *From Beachhead to Brittany*, p. 13.

110. *29 Let's Go, WWII G.I. Stories* (Paris: Stars and Stripes 1944-45), www.lonesentry.com/gi_stories_booklets/29thinfantry

111. *29 Let's Go, WWII G.I. Stories* (Paris: Stars and Stripes 1944-45), www.lonesentry.com/gi_stories_booklets/29thinfantry

112. Ewing, *29 Let's Go*, p. 124.

113. Balkoski, *From Beachhead to Brittany*, p. 42.

114. Gawne, *1944, Americans in Brittany*, p. 106; Balkoski, *From Beachhead to Brittany*, p. 51.

115. *After Action Report*, 29th Division, September 1944.

116. Balkoski, *From Beachhead to Brittany*, p. 69.

117. Balkoski, *From Beachhead to Brittany*, p. 70.

118. Ewing, *29 Let's Go*, p. 124; Balkoski, *From Beachhead to Brittany*, p. 72-73; Gawne, *1944, Americans in Brittany*, p. 106.

119. Gawne, *1944, Americans in Brittany*, p. 110.

120. *After Action Report*, 29th Division, September 1944.

121. *After Action Report*, 29th Division, September 1944.

122. Ewing, *29 Let's Go*, p. 136; *29 Let's Go, WWII G.I. Stories*

123. Balkoski, *From Beachhead to Brittany*, pp. 158-159.

124. Ewing, *29 Let's Go*, p. 136.

125. *After Action Report*, 29th Division, September 1944.

126. Gawne, *1944, Americans in Brittany*, pp. 106, 113.

127. Balkoski, *From Beachhead to Brittany*, pp. 183-184; Ewing, *29 Let's Go*, p. 141.

128. *After Action Report*, 29th Division, September 1944.

129. Balkoski, *From Beachhead to Brittany*, pp. 170, 185.

130. *After Action Report*, 29th Division, September 1944.

131. Gawne, *1944, Americans in Brittany*, p. 141.

132. Ewing, *29 Let's Go*, p. 141; Gawne, *1944, Americans in Brittany*, p. 141.

133. Balkoski, *From Beachhead to Brittany*, p. 267.

134. Balkoski, *From Beachhead to Brittany*, p. 280.

135. Martin Blumenson, *U.S. Army in World War II*, Chapter XXX The Battle for Brest, www.ibiblio.org/hyperwar/USA/USA-E-Breakout-30.html

136. Blumenson, *U.S. Army in World War II*.

CHAPTER 5

Somewhere in Germany

THE BROAD FRONT

While the 29th Division and other units of the American army were laying siege to Brest, the Supreme Allied Commander, General Eisenhower, was deciding on a strategy for invading the German homeland. The breakout from the Normandy beachhead had achieved rapid success after St. Lo was captured. Allied forces raced to the Seine River, liberated Paris, and pushed on to the borders of Germany.

The strategic debate among the Allied high command involved whether to invade Germany along a broad front or to direct Allied troops and resources in a single narrow thrust in an audacious effort to end the war by Christmas, if not before.

Key Allied commanders, most notably Bradley and Patton for the Americans, and Montgomery for the British, favored a single thrust approach. They differed, however, as to where to strike and which army should lead the assault.

Montgomery proposed seizing key bridges in Holland and across the Rhine to strike into the Ruhr valley and on to Berlin. He insisted that Allied resources be focused on this effort which came to be known as operation Market Garden.

Bradley, Patton and the Americans argued for a single thrust further south across the Rhine into the Saar valley and then on to Berlin.

Eisenhower saw value in both approaches, but logistics and supply shortages would not permit the Allies to do both to the extent desired by the generals. Cherbourg was the only usable Channel port in Allied possession, and most supplies and reinforcements were coming on to the Continent via the invasion beaches.

Prior to the Normandy invasion, Allied political leaders and their principal military advisors had vigorously debated the best strategy for defeating Germany. The U.S. Army's Chief of Staff and President Roosevelt's principal military advisor, General George Marshall, and most of his top subordinates, had favored an Allied invasion of Northwest Europe as the most direct and effective strategy for defeating the German army.

British Prime Minister Winston Churchill and his key military advisors, on the other hand, repeatedly urged a less direct assault on the German homeland. Churchill championed the invasion of North Africa, followed by the assault on Sicily, then an invasion of Italy, supposedly the "soft underbelly" of Europe. As the date for Overlord approached, Churchill proposed instead an attack in the Balkans which he believed would be less costly in lives and more politically beneficial by enabling U.S. and British forces to meet their Russian allies as far east in Europe as possible. Unlike FDR, Churchill foresaw political conflict with a victorious Soviet Union in the post-war world.

There were some Americans, like William Bullitt, a close advisor to Roosevelt, who agreed with Churchill's more political approach to Allied military strategy. In two memos written to FDR in early and mid 1943, Bullitt advised the President to invade the Balkans in an effort to forestall Soviet conquest and political control of central and eastern Europe. Roosevelt ignored Bullitt's advice, believing that he could persuade Stalin to join in his vision of a post-war world governed by the ideals of the Atlantic Charter and the United Nations.[1]

With the launching of Overlord, the establishment of the Normandy beachhead, and the breakout across France, Allied strategic unity temporarily returned. But the very success of the breakout produced new strategic opportunities that resulted once again in divisions among Allied military leaders.

Eisenhower has been accused of supporting Market Garden, which ultimately ended in failure, over the American plan which some historians claim had a better chance of success. Eisenhower's critics contend that his support of Montgomery's plan deprived Bradley and Patton of the necessary resources to breakthrough the still vulnerable Siegfried Line.

In his memoirs, General Bradley called Eisenhower's decision to support Market Garden "his gravest tactical error of the war." Market Garden, Bradley wrote, "was a massive assault *in the wrong direction* at what was probably the most crucial moment on the German front."[2]

British military historian H. Essame agreed with Bradley. Patton's Third Army, he wrote, was the perfect instrument at precisely the right place at precisely the right moment to pierce the Siegfried Line and drive on to Berlin. "The price to be paid for halting Patton," wrote Essame, ". . . would be heavy indeed.

Two-thirds of Allied casualties in the North-West Europe Campaign of 1944/45 were incurred after . . . September [1944]."[3]

British historian Max Hastings, in his recent study of the end of the war in Europe, calls the decision to favor Montgomery over his own commanders Eisenhower's "first serious error as ground commander," which resulted in closing the Allied "window of opportunity on the Western Front."[4]

Eisenhower has his defenders, too. John Ellis, for example, concludes that given the political and logistical constraints that the Supreme Commander operated under, there was "no real alternative to . . . [the] broad front advance."[5]

In truth, as B. H. Liddell Hart pointed out, Eisenhower's failure here was in attempting to accommodate as much as possible *both* Montgomery and Bradley/Patton. Eisenhower supported Market Garden but also directed Bradley's forces to advance as well.[6] In effect, Eisenhower chose a double thrust strategy, albeit one that gave the highest priority to Market Garden.[7]

Eisenhower's strategy was approved by President Roosevelt, Prime Minister Churchill, and the Combined Chiefs of Staff. In *Triumph and Tragedy*, the last volume of his history of the Second World War, Churchill recalled a meeting at the Quebec Conference where Admiral William Leahy read out to Churchill and Roosevelt the final report of the Combined Chiefs of Staff which approved "striking at the Ruhr and Saar," breaking the Siegfried Line and seizing "crossings over the Rhine."[8]

Most important for purposes of this book, however, were the consequences of the failure of Market Garden and the double thrust strategy. The Siegfried Line, which the Germans called the "Western Wall," was reinforced and strengthened along its whole front. The opportunity for a decisive, single thrust across the Rhine had evaporated. "[T]he last realistic prospect that the Allies might achieve a breakthrough to the heart of Germany," writes Max Hastings, "perished."[9] The Allied armies, including the Ninth Army, which now included the 29th Division as part of XIX Corps, would assault the Siegfried Line on a broad front, taking ground by costly attrition warfare. The fighting, wrote historian Charles B. MacDonald, would be "some of the most punishing of the war. It was a battle of the hedgerows all over again, only this time with the added misery of freezing rain, sleet, snow, flood, mud, pillboxes, and dense, dank woods straight out of frightening German folk tales."[10]

My father and the other soldiers of the 29th Division enjoyed a brief respite from battle after the capture of Brest. It did not, however, last very long. Beginning on September 24 and 25, the division moved by convoy and train through French towns and cities on its way to Holland, Belgium, and the German border. The trip covered more than 600 miles, and the soldiers were repeatedly cheered by French and Belgian citizens.[11]

The 29th Division assembled near Maastricht, Belgium, which was the headquarters area of General William Simpson's Ninth Army, on September 28-29. The Allied front facing the Siegfried Line was situated as follows: The Canadian First Army and the British Second Army, under General Montgomery, held the northernmost position near Nijmegen, Eindhoven, and across from Roermond;

the U.S. Ninth Army, including my father's division, was spread along an 11-mile front north and south of Maastricht, north of Aachen, across from Geilenkirchen, Julich, and Duren; the U.S. First Army, under General Hodges, was positioned south of the Ninth Army near Aachen, Malmedy, St. Vith, Bastogne, and Luxembourg; and the U.S. Third Army, under General Patton, held the southern sector across from the Moselle River.[12]

On September 29, 1944, for the first time since landing on Omaha Beach, my father's letter to his parents was from "Somewhere in Europe," instead of "Somewhere in France." This indicated that my father had left France and, perhaps, was on his way to Germany. In the letter, he noted that he was "lying in my tent," and was writing the letter "aided by a lantern." He expressed his belief that "when this European War is over us old timers stand a pretty good chance of getting out . . . ." In a second letter written that day, my father reflected a bit about France and the effect of army life on him. "I think I'll make a return visit to France after this mess is over," he wrote. "I shall always remember it as the land of bicycles and beautiful gals . . . ." "I guess I'll never be satisfied to settle down after this war," he continued, because the "army sure does give a wander lust."

The next day, again from "Somewhere in Europe," my father wrote that he was "being kept busy," and was "working hard but . . . feeling fine."

That same day, September 30, 1944, my father's division crossed the border into Germany.[13]

The weather that Fall and Winter of 1944 was "near record severity," with heavy rainfall, snow, and very cold temperatures.[14] In two letters written on October 1 and 2, my father mentioned the cold temperatures and noted that he "was forced to put on my winter drawers . . . ." He also mentioned that it was now "football days in the states."

THE SIEGFRIED LINE

The Siegfried Line, what the Germans called their "West Wall," was a series of strong and well-defended emplacements and pillboxes extending from the Dutch frontier to the Swiss border. The architects of these fortifications constructed them to complement the natural barriers of the Rhineland. Thus, where the natural barriers were the weakest, such as in the Belfort Gap, Aachen Plain and Moselle Valley, the fortifications were strongest.[15] By the time American commanders settled on the broad front strategy, the Siegfried Line was "three miles in depth," with "hundreds of mutually supporting pillboxes, troop shelters and command posts," and "pyramidal concrete projections called 'dragon's teeth,' draped in parallel rows . . . like some endless, scaly-backed reptile" to obstruct tanks.[16]

My father's division, as part of XIX Corps, was tasked with "seizing a bridgehead over the Roer River" at Julich.[17] This movement was also designed to pro

tect the left flank of the U.S. First Army. In this sector, the Siegfried Line fortifications extended across the entire front, and complemented the natural
barriers of the Wurm and Roer Rivers. German defenses included minefields,
barbed wire, anti-tank ditches, stone walls, and interlocking concrete pillboxes
where machine guns and anti-tank guns were placed.[18]

On October 1, my father's battalion engaged in "active patrolling," and positioned itself between Gangelt and Susterseel.[19] The next day, the division's
115th regiment conducted a diversionary attack and seized the towns of Hatterath, Birgden, and Kreuzrath.[20] The same day, my father's battalion of the 175th
"advanced approximately 1500 yards behind strong combat patrols."[21]

The After Action Report of the 115th regiment notes that on October 3, a battalion of the 175th "dispatched strong combat patrols toward Grilenkirchen,
maintaining pressure upon the enemy situated there," while the 115th attacked
Niederheide where it ran into "a heavy concentration of enemy small-arms and
mortar fire . . . ."[22]

The next day, my father's battalion established a bridgehead across Saeffler
Creek. [23] Against tough enemy resistance, which resulted in 61 casualties, my
father's battalion captured Breberen on the north bank of the creek.[24]

During and after this action on October 4 and 5, my father got nostalgic in letters to his parents. "Tomorrow," he wrote on October 4, "is an anniversary for
me for it was two years ago that I left for overseas . . . ." "[T]he past two years,"
he continued, "have been full of experiences . . . ." And the next day: "Well its
been two years ago today I left the states. Won't know how to behave when I get
back."

On October 6, my father's battalion went into temporary division reserve. That
day he wrote to his parents that a friend of his who was stationed in New York
said he was sick of the war. My father sarcastically remarked, "Must be tough
having to serve in New York City."

That same day, the Commander of XIX Corps, Major General Charles Corlett,
visited the 29th Division headquarters and ordered the division's infantry regiments to continue to probe the Siegfried Line and to be ready to exploit opportunities created by the advance of the 2nd Armored Division near Geilenkirchen.[25]

On October 7, the 175th regiment conducted an early morning raid on German
positions near Hatterath, in an unsuccessful effort to set on fire the woods
nearby the enemy positions.[26] That same day, my father wrote that he was "now
somewhere in Germany." "Saw Paris, quite a bit of France, Belgium, and Holland," he wrote. This was the first of his wartime letters that had his return address as "Somewhere in Germany."

He also informed his parents in that letter that he sent them a news clipping
"of the Brest campaign." "Its no secret," he wrote, ". . . as it has been officially
announced that we took part in that campaign." "Everyday," he continued,
"brings us a bit nearer to our destination. Then it will be what we are all looking
forward to, home sweet home."

It was also on October 7, 1944, that Lt. Col. William Purnell, commander of

the 175th regiment, recommended in a memo to the Commanding General of the
29th Division that "Frank Fabian Sempa . . . be appointed a temporary Junior
Grade Warrant Officer." The basis for the recommendation, wrote Lt. Col Purnell, included that Sgt. Sempa's performance of his duties has been
"Excellent," and "[h]is character is Excellent." "Sgt. Sempa," concluded Purnell, "has at all times demonstrated superior leadership, courage and
performed his duties in a superior manner."[27] The memo also noted the dates
that my father was inducted into the army (April 25, 1941) and promoted (corporal on April 15, 1942; sergeant on May 1, 1942; and staff sergeant on September 15, 1942).

During most of the remainder of October, my father's regiment, and indeed
most of the 29th Division, enjoyed a period of relative inactivity. There were patrols and several raids, but the division did not engage in large-scale offensive
action. The After Action Report for October 1944 characterizes this activity as
"active defense."[28]

Units of the division conducted raids on Schierwaldenrath, Bauchem, Bu-
scherheide, Niederheide, Waldenrath and a wooded area near Hatterath. "These
raids," explained Joseph Ewing, "had no object other than that of inflicting casualties, taking prisoners, and keeping the enemy on edge."[29] The raids kept
pressure on German forces so that troops could not be diverted to other sectors
where American attacks were in progress.[30]

In a letter dated October 9, 1944, my father informed his parents that he received a letter from his brother Eddie, who was in France. "If I ever get within
striking distance of him," my father wrote, "I'm surely going to look him up."

Writing by candlelight from his foxhole in Germany on October 14, my father
mentioned that he "sure would like to get into a soft comfortable bed." He noted
that he had pork chops for supper and was still regularly receiving copies of the
Scranton Tribune. He remarked that "vacation time is almost over back home,"
and that he hardly knows "how to spell the word vacation anymore."

Two days later in a letter, my father explained that he was living in a "dugout." He mentioned eating a good meal consisting of steak, mashed potatoes,
gravy, green peas, bread and butter, coffee, and peaches a few days later. He also noted that he saw a movie, "Show Business," starring Eddie Cantor, and that
it was the "first show I've seen in ages." In another letter that month, he mentioned seeing Bing Crosby in "Going My Way."

In a letter dated October 26, 1944, my father mentioned that he had sent his
parents an article that appeared in *Stars and Stripes* "all about the Brest Campaign, which we participated in." He asked his parents to save the article because he'll "be able to relate some fine stories." Three days later, he noted that
he sent them Dutch money and other items as souvenirs, and wrote, "Someday
when this is all over I'll have some fine stories to tell about each souvenir."

There was no escape from the war, however. Virtually every day and night,
enemy artillery and mortar shells disturbed the relative peace. In several letters
written in late October and early November, my father expressed hope that he
could sleep or write letters if "Jerry doesn't interrupt too much."

The After Action Report for October 1944 contained some battle lessons learned by the veterans of the fighting in France and Germany. First, combat units when clearing villages and towns should avoid the tendency to break into small groups. Houses should be entered, if necessary, with significant numbers and force so that the enemy cannot defeat small groups in detail. Second, an area cannot be properly defended from within houses, where small groups of soldiers can be surrounded, isolated, and defeated. Third, combat patrols need good communications equipment so they can call for artillery fire when necessary. Fourth, mortar fire provides invaluable assistance to combat patrols. Fifth, sometimes small units must be able to operate independently.[31]

These battle lessons would prove to be relevant and important to the soldiers of the 29th Division as they prepared for their next assignment which involved attacking toward Julich over terrain dotted with numerous villages and towns.

NOVEMBER OFFENSIVE

At a war council in Brussels on October 18, 1944, General Eisenhower decided to launch a November offensive toward the Rhine along the broad front of the Siegfried Line.[32] The Ninth Army, including the 29th Division, was ordered to attack along an 11-mile front on the First Army's northern flank toward Julich.[33]

The timing of the offensive depended on the weather because the plan called for the Eighth Air Force to soften-up German positions.[34] November's weather proved to be miserable as it rained all but two days that month.[35]

While my father's division prepared for the offensive, an "intensive training program was also carried on, stressing battle drills with special emphasis being placed on tank-infantry-tank-destroyer training."[36] Each division unit held "demonstrations" to explain and help visualize new methods and procedures.[37] Some of the division's units conducted reconnaissance patrols in German-held territory.[38]

November 1944 was also presidential election time in the United States. President Roosevelt was running for an unprecedented fourth term against Republican Thomas E. Dewey. The American military command made use of the upcoming election as codes for postponing or launching the offensive. "The Republicans are winning" meant postponement. "It's a Democratic landslide" meant the offensive was on.[39]

On November 2, my father mentioned in a letter that he had attended Mass on All Saints Day, had a shower and a change of clothes, and was going to have pork chops for supper. The next day, he wrote that his brother Eddie "is around somewhere nearby I think." My father indicated that he was going to attempt to locate Eddie. In another letter on November 5, my father again noted that he was "trying to locate Eddie."

On November 5, troops from the 115th and 175th regiments were ordered to relieve the 2nd Armored Division, and this occurred the next day. The 115th was positioned southeast of Bettendorf, east of Baesweiler, and northeast of Oidtweiler. The 175th filled-in south and southwest of the 115th near Oidtweiler and Schaufenberg.[40]

The weather and German artillery were ever present. On November 6, my father wrote that he intended to go to bed early that night and he hoped "Jerry doesn't interrupt too much." The next day, he noted that "Winter has set in and its going to be a rugged season." He complained that his feet were cold.

In that November 7 letter, my father's thoughts turned briefly to the presidential election in the states. "Should know sometime tomorrow how the election came out," he wrote.

My father wrote two letters on November 8. In the first letter, he noted that he "was to a GI show tonight and it was good. A bit of mental relaxation to say the least." He also noted that he had donuts and coffee courtesy of the Red Cross clubmobile. He assured his parents that "Everything with me is o.k."

In the second letter, my father mentioned that it was "getting close to 10 o'clock and my bed time. Barring too many interruptions from Jerry I should sleep until 7." He noted that he'd been drinking a lot of coffee because you "have to have something to keep warm." He mentioned that it was going to be a tough winter season ahead, he was working "steady," and was still looking for his brother Eddie.

Back in the United States, FDR was reelected to his fourth term as President. In a November 9 letter to his parents, my father wrote: "Heard of FDR's election and it bore out my prediction that a change at this time was uncalled for." He also mentioned that the weather was "miserable" all day, and that he intended to get to bed early. "Hope Jerry doesn't interrupt to spoil my sleep."

As preparations continued for the offensive, General Eisenhower visited the 29th Division on November 10.[41] Throughout the war, Eisenhower made a practice of visiting some of the frontline troops prior to sending them into battle. It was a leadership style that endeared the Supreme Commander to his men.

The next day, November 11, my father reminded his parents in a letter that it was "Armistice Day," the anniversary of the end of the First World War. He noted that he was "being kept busy," and that the "weather continues to be rugged."

On November 13, my father wrote that he was in his "dugout," and planned to write a few letters "barring any interruptions from Jerry." He also noted that he "voted for FDR."

The next day, he wrote two letters to his parents, noting that the weather was bad again, he was eating well ("meat loaf, potatoes, gravy, corn, pickled red beets, coffee, and fruit salad"), and received their packages which contained fruitcake and cookies.

On November 15, again commenting on the miserable weather, my father wrote that "the glamour of living in mud is fast fading."

On November 16, General Gerhardt received word that the offensive was on. The weather had cleared just enough to allow the air corps to do its work. The

29th Division's attack was preceded by a two-hour air bombardment. Medium and heavy bombers targeted Aldenhoven and Julich. Tactical air forces bombed the smaller villages and towns along the division front.[42] More than ten thousand tons of bombs were dropped by more than four thousand planes.[43] The division attacked into the Roer plain from positions near Baesweiler and Oidtweiler. Much of the terrain on which the soldiers would fight was low and flat, though there were patches of high ground that surrounded the numerous towns and villages.[44]

Historian Russell Weigley notes that the German defenders of the Roer transformed every town and village into a "menacing fortress." My father's division faced a defensive web of trenches, minefields, anti-tank ditches, artillery emplacements, mortars, and machine guns manned by infantry clustered in cellars throughout the villages and towns. "Across the Roer plain," writes Weigley, "the villages and towns were so numerous that they readily formed . . . a great network of mutually supporting fortifications." What is more, the American attackers faced "the most powerful German reserve immediately behind the front anywhere north of the Ardennes."[45]

The 29th Division's commander, General Gerhardt, was considered by some of his colleagues as "the best combat commander in the European Theater."[46] Gerhardt's strategy in the Roer plain was to avoid direct attacks on the village and town strongpoints, seize the areas around them to isolate the German defenders, and cut their communications.[47] The division's After Action Report notes that Gerhardt's strategy derived in part from lessons learned from the fighting in France, especially at Vire, which taught that "capturing a town without first taking the high ground dominating it was usually a costly operation."[48]

In war, however, as the great theorist Carl von Clausewitz wrote, plans and strategies seldom survive contact with the enemy. Gerhardt's strategy did not account for the fact that, as Weigley notes, the towns and villages of the Roer plain "were too numerous and thus too close together to permit safe infiltration between them."[49]

THE ROER PLAIN

My father's regiment (175th) and the 115th led the division's attack on November 16, with the 116th initially in reserve.[50] The initial targets of the attack were the areas near Bettendorf and Siersdorf. My father's regiment attacked from Oidtweiler and Neuweiler and made limited progress against tough enemy resistance. Some of the regiment, after advancing a few hundred yards, were pinned down in an irrigation ditch by enemy fire from a railroad embankment and a nearby village.[51]

In a letter written on the first day of the offensive, my father noted that both the weather and the fighting were "rugged." He complained that his feet were cold, and expressed longing for "a warm house."

The limited advance on the first day of the offensive caused General Gerhardt to alter his strategy of avoiding direct attacks on towns and villages.[52] But the second day's attacks fared little better than the first. On that day, the division's 115th and 116th regiments attacked toward Setterich, but met heavy resistance.[53] The 175th continued its attack toward Siersdorf and Bettendorf. On that day, my father simply noted in a letter that the weather continued to be bad and his feet continued to be cold.

By the evening of November 17, my father's regiment was "dug into the wet ground for protection from the artillery and the cold" in front of Bettendorf and Siersdorf.[54] That evening, Ewing notes, heavy rain fell, "soaking the battlefields and drenching the troops in their uncovered foxholes."[55]

The next day, the 29th Division's attack made considerable progress. The 175th took Bettendorf, and my father's battalion launched an attack to seize the nearby town of Schleiden against strong enemy resistance.[56]

My father's battalion took Schleiden on November 19, and the town's seizure demonstrated successful techniques for assaulting village strongpoints. First, the battalion had machine gun and mortar support from nearby villages (in this instance, Bettendorf). Second, artillery was concentrated on a single objective: the village or town strongpoint. Third, my father's battalion received sufficient support from the 747th Tank Battalion.[57] The After Action Report characterized my father's battalion's seizure of Schleiden as "a beautifully coordinated tank-infantry movement."[58]

On November 20, after its successful seizure of Schleiden, my father's battalion moved southeast against Niedermenz, and occupied the town by the end of the morning.[59] About 300 German prisoners were captured, most from cellars.[60]

In two letters written on November 19 and 20, my father told his parents that "the going is rugged." He noted that his feet were wet and cold, and that he hoped to get some sleep "barring any interruptions from Jerry."

On November 21, the 1st and 2nd battalions of the 175th attacked toward Aldenhoven, an important road center on the way to Julich. After securing Niedermenz by repelling enemy attacks launched from the nearby town of Putzdorf, my father's battalion joined in that effort by attacking toward the crucial road network southwest of Aldenhoven.[61] That day, my father wrote that he was "being kept very busy," and had "little time" to do anything else but fight. The next day, my father wrote that "someone just mentioned that tomorrow is Thanksgiving Day." He noted, however, that "Holidays don't mean a thing these days."

The final defensive arc before the Roer River and Julich were the towns of Bourheim, Koslar, and Kirchberg.[62] German defenders in all three towns put up fierce resistance and launched repeated counterattacks against the 29th Division's infantry regiments and support units.

My father's regiment attacked Bourheim, with the 2nd battalion initially meeting scattered resistance, resulting in two platoons entering part of the town.[63] This small force, however, came under heavy enemy fire and was pushed out of the town.[64] The next day, two battalions of the 175th, the 1st battalion and my father's battalion, launched another attack on Bourheim. The 1st battalion attacked from the north and northwest, while my father's battalion attacked from the south.[65]

On November 23, both battalions conducted "mopping up" operations. The 1st battalion covered the northern sector of Bourheim and advanced to the eastern side of town where it was met by small-arms, mortar, and artillery fire, and tanks. My father's battalion covered the southern sector of the town and encountered stiff opposition as it advanced toward the western side of town.[66] At one point, two German tanks fired at my father's battalion's position from directly opposite its front, until the tanks were chased away by artillery and tanks from the 747th Tank Battalion.[67]

During each of the next three days, the Germans counterattacked with heavy artillery, mortar, and small-arms fire, tanks, and even air power.[68] The After Action Report noted that the 175th regiment "experienced a rough day on 24 November. The enemy maintained constant pressure on Bourheim and fire from mortar, small-arms and especially artillery was severe."[69]

Each day the Germans shelled the town, then brought up tanks and infantry to attempt to push the 175th out of Bourheim, and each day my father's regiment, with artillery, air, and tank support, valiantly fought off the attacks.[70]

On November 25 and 26, the German attacks were preceded by air bombardment of Bourheim. On November 26, the enemy sent in 500 infantry troops, six tanks, and a self-propelled gun, but the 175th, again with air support, held its ground and drove off the enemy.[71] The After Action Report credits my father's battalion and the 2nd battalion of the 175th with doing "an heroic job" that day.[72]

After three days of brutal combat to seize and hold Bourheim, the 175th moved back to division reserve near Siersdorf and Durboslar.[73]

Joseph Ewing notes that the 175th's three-day struggle for Bourheim involved the "heaviest artillery concentrations sustained by the [29th] Division at any time during the war."[74] Historian Charles B. MacDonald reflected that while Bourheim was hard to take, "it was even more difficult to hold . . . [against] a three-day siege of counterattacks . . . preceded by intense shelling."[75]

My father's letters during the struggle for Bourheim give some hint of the intensity of the fighting. On November 23, he mentioned eating a Thanksgiving Day dinner, but also noted that "the going is rugged." He expressed the hope of getting some sleep "if Jerry doesn't interrupt." The next day, he again noted in a letter that "the going is rugged."

Four days later on November 28, my father wrote: "Have been very busy the last couple of days so was unable to write." He mentioned again that it was "rugged over here." The next day, he told his parents that he was "Being kept on the go all the time," and lamented that there would be "[n]o furlough for me until this mess is over."

My father's November 30 letter indicates that things had settled down a bit. He mentioned receiving an early Christmas card and that he saw a movie. This letter was addressed from "Somewhere in Germany and Berlin Bound."

By the end of November, the After Action Report notes that "the Division was preparing for . . . the crossing of the ROER river." The Roer, the Report continued, "was the last major barrier in front of the Rhine and it would open the way for a drive across the Cologne plain to the heart of Germany."[76]

But before the division could cross the Roer, small pockets of enemy strongpoints on the outskirts of Julich would have to be cleared.[77]

November was a costly month for the 29th Division and my father's regiment. The division as a whole suffered 1,883 casualties, including 382 killed, that month. My father's regiment suffered 750 casualties, including 159 killed.[78]

During the first eight days of December, the 116th and 115th regiments fought to eliminate the remaining small strongpoints around Julich, including a concrete sports stadium called the Sportplatz, a swimming pool about 200 yards from the stadium, and a group of brick farm buildings known as the Hasenfeld Gut.[79]

My father's regiment, meanwhile, occupied Bourheim and secured Kirchberg. This activity included aggressive patrolling along the Roer River. Some units engaged in training, including river-crossing tactics and techniques. The division's zone during this time was subjected to strafing and bombing from German planes.[80]

While the Ninth Army slugged its way to the Roer north of Aachen, to the south, the General Hodge's First Army fought the bitter Battle of the Huertgen Forest, which General Bradley called "sheer butchery on both sides."[81] Further south, Patton's Third Army struggled toward the Moselle and Metz, while General Patch's Seventh Army advanced towards Nancy, Luneville, Strasbourg, and Saarbrucken.[82]

By December 9 along the 29th Division's front, the west bank of the Roer was cleared of the enemy. It was still not safe, however, to cross the river because of the Roer dams.

There were seven dams in all, two major ones and five lesser ones, located south of the Huertgen Forest.[83] These dams, as Max Hastings notes, "offered the Germans scope to flood the low ground at will."[84] If the Ninth Army troops, including my father's division, attempted to cross the Roer, the Germans could flood the river and thereby isolate on the east bank smaller units which crossed the river. This would enable the Germans repeatedly to defeat in detail portions of the Ninth Army and prevent the Americans from exploiting the crossing of the river. Thus, the dams had to be taken or destroyed before the Ninth Army could cross the Roer. Efforts to seize the dams by ground forces and to destroy them by air bombardment failed into mid-December 1944. By that time, there was another reason to delay the crossing of the Roer--the beginning of Hitler's last great offensive through the lightly defended Ardennes Forest known to history as the Battle of the Bulge.

WINTER INTERLUDE

Throughout much of December 1944, my father's division held its position on the west bank of the Roer River. Other than patrolling, there were no significant offensive actions by the 29th Division, and the Germans across the river did not launch any significant attacks.

On December 1, my father wrote to his parents that he was well and "being kept plenty busy." He also noted that he was actively searching for the whereabouts of his brother Eddie. That same day he sent his parents a Christmas card that said, "The 29th Infantry Division on its way through the Siegfried Line, wishes you a very Merry Christmas. 29 Let's Go."

The next day, he wrote that he "spent the last two hours trying to locate Eddie. And have a general idea where he might be." He mentioned that he had pork chops for supper and that it was "getting close to bedtime." "If Jerry doesn't interrupt," he concluded, "I should get a good night's rest."

On December 3, 1944, my father wrote to inform his parents that he found and talked to his brother Eddie. "Got good news for you today," he exclaimed. "Saw Eddie today and let me tell you he is looking swell." "Found out his whereabouts this morning," he continued. "Permission to go was gladly given and a jeep furnished. Had no difficulty finding him . . . He was tickled pink to see me. Spent about 3 hours with him. Talked about most everything under the sun." Shortly thereafter, a news story appeared in the *Scranton Tribune* about the Sempa brothers meeting in Germany in the midst of the war.

On December 5 and 6, my father told his parents about a rotation plan being put into effect for furloughs for some of the troops. "Heard today that they are starting to send some men home, on furlough, from this theatre," he wrote in the first letter. "Don't look for me, though, until this mess is over." In the second letter, he wrote that "the rotation plan went into effect in this theatre today with a number of men on their way home for 30 day furloughs. That will get them home for X-mas, lucky guys." "Don't expect me home," he wrote, "until this mess is over."

In a December 10 letter, my father identified the specific corps and army that oversaw his division. "Censorship now permits us to state," he wrote, "we are in the 19th Corps of the Ninth Army . . . ." The next day, he told his parents that he watched a movie starring Gary Cooper. Two days later, he wrote that he saw an old friend from Avoca and spent several hours with him. He also mentioned that he was leaving for Paris the next day on a pass.

My father returned from Paris on December 22. Meanwhile, the XIX Corps was divided, with the 30th Division and the 2nd Armored Division being pulled from the Ninth Army and moved south to help stop the German counteroffensive in the bulge. This meant that the 29th Division had the responsibility of holding the line formerly held by the entire XIX Corps.[85]

By December 20, the division was positioned along the Roer River as follows: the 3rd and 2nd battalions of the 116th regiment on the left; the 2nd and 3rd battalions of the 175th regiment in the center; and the 17th Calvary squadron on the right. The 115th was in division reserve.[86] The entire division was now placed in XIII Corps.

The division's task in what was termed the "quiet" sector, was to establish a strong defense over a 12-mile front "using the terrain and all available forces."[87] This meant a defense in depth, using the captured towns and villages of the Roer plain as mutually-supporting strongpoints, just like the Germans did. "Each town in the Division area," states the After Action Report, "was wired in. Emplacements were dug to cover all possible approaches. All tanks and tank-destroyers on line were dug-in and mutually supporting as far as possible." Also, communication trenches ran from perimeter defenses into each town. "This made it possible for the defenders as a last ditch resort to conduct house-to-house fighting."[88]

Although in the "quiet" sector of the front, my father's division was subjected to German bombing and strafing missions during December.[89]

On December 22, my father wrote letters to his parents and brother Johnnie. He informed them that he had spent five days in Paris and "saw most everything of any importance." He mentioned that he had a "swell time" there and took many photographs which he will send home "when they are developed." In one letter, he enclosed a religious medal he got in Notre Dame, and said that he sent a separate package to them containing perfume, powder, and Rosaries from Paris. He urged his parents not to sell the car because "I'll be needing it when I get home in '45." He also mentioned that he will be sending home his Combat Infantryman's Badge, which he recently was awarded.

On December 24, he wrote two letters. "Here it is X-mas Eve, the third spent overseas. . . . Its far from any X-mas I've had so far but I'm thankful to be here to spend it. For certain we will all be together by next X-mas . . . ." He concluded the letter by writing, "Hope tomorrow is a day of happiness to you and Dad. Be thankful we are all alive, even though not together."

In the second Christmas Eve letter, my father waxed eloquent about the meaning of Christmas. "Things so far are quiet on X-mas Eve," he noted. "Just finished decorating a X-mas tree and it sure does look good." He continued, "Of course surroundings aren't the best here in war torn Germany but we are making the best of it." "Before the night is over," he explained, "the guys intend to sing a few X-mas carols. Tomorrow is just another day in this war but that certain something will be there in everyone's heart." He said he was "sure that it won't be very long into 1945 that this whole mess will be over and a good deal of us destined to return home." He concluded with this Christmas wish: "Hope today and tomorrow are happy days in your lives. Rejoice in that we are all enjoying good health though circumstances do not permit a reunion."

In his Christmas Day letter, my father wrote: "Just finished X-mas dinner and it was wonderful." He mentioned that he ate turkey, gravy, potatoes, cranberry sauce, coffee, pumpkin pie, and "a surprise package." "It was one of the best X-mas dinners we had in my four X-mas' in the army."

The After Action Report notes that "Christmas trees were in abundance" on

Christmas Day along the 29th Division's front. "All of the Division enjoyed turkey dinner." The Report further noted that "the Commanding General visited
each [battalion] in the Division . . . ." Religious services were held in "all units
throughout the Division." The Report noted that even in enemy-controlled Julich
across the river church bells rang to celebrate Christmas.[90]

On December 30, my father wrote that "the weather here is very cold." "1944
runs out tomorrow," he noted. "Wonder what 1945 is going to bring." His New
Year's Eve letter noted that the "present year sure has been an eventful one . . .
Hope to be seeing you in 1945."

In his first letter of 1945, written on New Year's Day, my father was optimistic. "Am starting the New Year right," he wrote. "Slept the New Year in for
there wasn't anything else to do." He explained that, "Someone did awaken me
at midnight with New Year wishes but all I remember is rolling over and going
back to sleep . . . ." He confidently predicted, "I'll be seeing you and Dad in
1945, you may be sure of that. Well I haven't got far to go to my final destination. Have seen the leading capitals of the world, namely Washington, London,
Paris and I'll see Berlin!"

January was a relatively inactive month for my father's division as it secured
and defended its line along the west bank of the Roer River. The Roer dams
remained in German hands. The Battle of the Bulge was still raging. Until the
dams were seized or destroyed, and the German counteroffensive defeated, the
29th Division remained in place, across the river from Julich.

In early January, the 116th and 175th regiments "occupied front line positions," while the 115th was in reserve.[91] On January 4, my father reminded his
parents that he was in the Ninth Army, and noted that he was "busy all day."
The next day, he again wrote that he was "being kept busy."

On January 6, my father mentioned in a letter that he heard on the radio that
"they are thinking of drafting nurses. Sure must be a shortage . . . ." He noted
that "the radio was playing 'It Had to be You,' and it is lovely." He finished the
letter by writing, "And so to bed. Hope Jerry doesn't interrupt." The next day, he
wrote that he "was busy all day."

One thing that kept my father and the other men busy was organizing and
strengthening the towns in the "immediate rear" for defense.[92] Each regiment
was responsible for several towns. The 115th was assigned to Siersdorf, Durboslar, Aldenhoven, and Emelsdorf. The 116th organized the defense of Friealdenhoven, Koslar, and two nearby towns. My father's regiment was responsible for
the defense of Pattern, Bourheim, Kirchberg, Altdorf, Inden, Pier, and Schopho-
ven.[93]

The soldiers of the 29th also "conducted a harvesting program," which was intended to interdict enemy movements, deprive the enemy of rest, deceive the
enemy as to division's intentions and plans, and conserve strength.[94]

Throughout January and into February, the division sent about 60 patrols
across the Roer.[95] Some patrols skirmished with the Germans; some entered minefields and engaged in fire fights; and some never engaged the enemy.[96] Other
combat patrols took prisoners and attempted to destroy enemy outposts on

the east side of the river.[97] Another reason for conducting the patrols was "to maintain the aggressive spirit" of the division.[98]

The division also launched three major raids across the Roer in January. On January 8, units of the 116th regiment conducted a raid designed to destroy Pickartzhof Castle, just north of Julich. Eighty-four men crossed the river in 16 rubber boats in heavy snow. The men got lost, never located the castle, but found their way back across the river to the division line.[99]

The second raid took place on January 14, and involved 89 men of my father's regiment in an effort to take prisoners and destroy buildings south of Julich.[100] As the men attempted to cross the river, the Germans "laid down heavy mortar and machine gun fire," and blew a whistle which caused the raiding party to return to the west bank without ever making it across the river. The Germans had accidentally stumbled on the signal (blowing the whistle) for the raiding party's retreat.[101]

Near the end of January, 54 soldiers of the 116th regiment crossed the river in an effort to raid Broicherhaus, a mansion north of Julich, in order to seize prisoners. The raiding party became embroiled in a fire fight near the mansion and had to withdraw.

There were other minor raids and constant patrolling and reconnaissance missions throughout the month. "[A]lmost every night a patrol would cross the river to reconnoiter the German position" east of the Roer.[102]

When the soldiers were not patrolling or participating in a raid, there was not much to do. "Instead of fighting," writes Charles Whiting, "the GIs spent cold, boring days improving their billets, keeping warm, and dreaming up new ways of preparing their 'K' and 'C' canned rations."[103] "It was only . . . the occasional bursts of offensive activity for the front line troops," Joseph Ewing explained, "that relieved the Blue-and-Gray soldier from the dull daily sameness of his army detail."[104]

On January 15, my father wrote to his parents that, "Everything with me is o.k. Not working too hard." The next day, he mentioned getting coffee and doughnuts from the Red Cross clubmobile.

It was also in mid January, that the Soviet Union launched a major offensive on the Eastern Front in East Prussia and Poland, toward Upper Silesia and Czechoslovakia, and Hungary. The Red Army advanced up to 40 miles per day on its drive to the Oder River.[105]

In a letter dated January 17, 1945, my father noted the developments on the Eastern Front. "News from the Russian front today is good," he wrote, "and very likely to hasten the end of this war."

On January 21, my father sent his parents a "large sheet containing the exploits of the XIX Corps since D-Day." He asked them to "save it and I'll explain it to you when I get home."

Six days later, my father noted that he "had a bottle of Coca Cola for the first time in ages." (Joseph Ewing in his history of the 29th Division, noted that it was in January that the "Coca Cola ration began to appear" on the division's front. It was, Ewing wrote, "an unbelievable luxury, to be sipped slowly and raved over.").[106] My father also mentioned that "Stars and Stripes has announced that starting next month furloughs to England are in store." He wrote that he was "hopeful of hitting the furlough plan back to the states," and noted that "a few of the boys have left for 30 days at home."

In late January, the 29th Division was positioned along the Roer as follows: the 116th regiment's 1st and 2nd battalions defended the left sector of the front, with its 3rd battalion in reserve at Friealdenhoven; the 115th, with one battalion of the 175th, covered the right sector of the front; the remaining units of the 175th were in reserve in Pattern. Emplacements and other defenses were strengthened and improved, while "plans for future offensive action were in the process of formulation."[107]

By the end of January 1945, the Americans, having suffered more than 80,000 casualties, won the Battle of the Bulge. It was "the most costly battle the Americans fought in north-west Europe."[108] Hitler's last gamble in the West had ended in disaster. Soviet forces were advancing in the East. The Third Reich's days appeared to be numbered. In a January 31 letter to his parents, my father summed-up the situation: "War news today is very good."

OPERATION GRENADE

The U.S. Ninth Army was shifted to the 21st Army Group under the overall command of British General Montgomery. Montgomery and the British Chiefs of Staff favored a renewal of the offensive farther north toward the Ruhr region. Bradley and Patton, on the other hand, wanted the major push further south toward the Eifel Forest, and led by the U.S. First and Third Armies.[109]

Once again, battlefield successes created opportunities and renewed the strategic debate between proponents of the broad-front strategy and those favoring a more directed single thrust into the heart of Germany. The British Chiefs "told their American counterparts that there must be only one major thrust and that overwhelming strength must be concentrated into it."[110]

President Roosevelt, Prime Minister Churchill, and the Combined Chiefs of Staff met on Malta in late January-early February 1945 to discuss the next offensive in the West. In his history of the Second World War, Churchill recalled that the British Chiefs "doubted whether we were strong enough for two great simultaneous operations, and felt that the northern advance by Montgomery's Twenty-First Army Group would be much more important."[111] Churchill wrote that "the matter was keenly argued by the Combined Chiefs of Staff."[112] That was putting it mildly. In his memoirs, General Bradley describes a bitter argument between the British and American Chiefs over the best strategy for driving to the Rhine River. Bradley wrote that at one meeting in Malta, British General Alan Brooke, Churchill's top military adviser, "viciously attacked [Eisenhower's] plan." Bradley also described a "very acid meeting," where GeneralMarshall leaped to Eisenhower's defense. He noted that Marshall later recalled the Malta discussions as a "terrible session which quickly devolved into scathing criticisms of personalities."[113]

Historian Max Hastings writes that the strategy debated at Malta "caused some of the most bitter arguments of the war." General Marshall at one point in the discussions threatened to resign if the British Chiefs "did not fall into line."[114]

In the end, just as he had done in the Fall campaign, Eisenhower decided on a broad front strategy, but accorded the highest priority and most resources to Montgomery's northern offensive.[115] The first phase of the offensive would be a Canadian First Army attack from Nijmegen to the southeast, codenamed Operation Veritable. Simultaneously, the U.S. First Army would seize or destroy the Roer dams and the U.S. Ninth Army would cross the Roer River, seize Julich and other east bank towns, and advance northeast toward the Rhine. This operation was codenamed Grenade. The next phase, codenamed Operation Lumberjack, would have the U.S. First and Third Armies attack toward Cologne and the Koblenz area. Then, Sixth Army Group under General Devers would attack south of the Moselle, an operation codenamed Undertone. Finally, General Montgomery would make the main effort to cross the Rhine, codenamed Operation Plunder.[116]

My father's division as part of the Ninth Army was now attached to Montgomery's 21st Army Group and, therefore, would take part in the major thrust toward the Rhine.

The 29th Division's After Action Report notes that at the beginning of February planning and training commenced for shifting from defense to an advance across the Roer and beyond. "The month of January," the Report states, "had seen the 29th Infantry Division conduct an organized defense in depth on the west bank" of the Roer. "This was necessitated," the Report continues, "by the enemy offensive in the 'bulge' area and the consequent shift of troops to the south to meet this threat."[117]

On February 1, my father wrote an optimistic letter to his parents. "The war news today is good." "Maybe," he continued, "it will be over soon." Early that month, the 29th Division shifted back from XIII Corps to XIX Corps, but remained in the Ninth Army.[118] All units of XIX Corps began regrouping and training "in preparation for the projected offensive operation."[119]

My father's division planned and trained for crossing the Roer River, seizing and occupying Julich, and exploiting any success to the north and east toward the Rhine River.[120] Initially, a battalion of my father's regiment was ordered to conduct a raid across the Roer, capture an ancient fortress in Julich called the Citadel (believed to be an enemy command post), and reconnoiter Julich to estimate the strength of its defenders. The raid was unexpectedly cancelled.[121]

With units returning from the Bulge, XIX Corps now fielded the 29th, 30th and 83rd Infantry Divisions, the 2nd Armored Division, and the all important support units.[122]

The date for launching Operation Grenade was February 10, weather permitting and assuming the seizure or destruction of the Roer dams. On February 5, my father's battalion of the 175th relieved a 115th battalion and the entire 175th regiment occupied the sector of the front from the Aldenhoven-Julich road to a railroad bridge south of Julich.[123]

In a February 8 letter, my father responded to receiving news of the death of a soldier he knew from back home. "Too bad about [him]," my father wrote, "but such are the fortunes of war." For combat soldiers like my father, who had been waging war against the enemy in tough battle after tough battle since Omaha Beach, death was a routine occurrence, to be lamented but also to be expected. The carnage and destructiveness of war obviously had transformed the young newspaper correspondent into a battle-hardened combat sergeant focused on his job to help defeat the enemy and hopefully get home as soon as possible.

On February 9, one day before the offensive was to start, my father noted in a letter that he was "plenty busy all day . . . ."

That day the offensive was postponed for two reasons. First, heavy rain continued to fall, flooding parts of the Roer River. Second, the Germans still controlled the Roer dams, and had blown the largest of the dams to flood the entire river along the Ninth Army's front.[124]

Eisenhower, much to Bradley's chagrin, ordered the First U.S. Army to shift its priority from an offensive toward the Eifel to capturing the Roer dams.[125] The dams were in American hands when the Ninth Army launched its offensive.

Operation Veritable, the Canadian First Army's offensive, went off as scheduled on February 8. It was not until two weeks later that Operation Grenade was launched by the Ninth Army

Operation Grenade was to be a massive offensive involving eleven divisions, including the 29th, with a total of almost 400,000 troops (including VII Corps) and "the largest concentration of guns an American army had yet gathered for an offensive on the Western Front."[126]

Charles MacDonald writes of Operation Grenade that the "Ninth Army was preparing a paralyzing blow that would turn out to be . . . one of the most powerful setpiece attacks launched by an American force in World War II."[127] This massive attack would take place along a relatively narrow 12-mile front.

Joseph Ewing noted that XIX Corps of the Ninth Army was tasked with launching the main effort to cross the Roer, and that the 29th Division was to lead that effort for XIX Corps. The significance of the 29th's role in the planned attack was evidenced by a February 18 visit to the division's command at the 175th's command post in Aldenhoven by Generals Bradley, Simpson (Commander of Ninth Army) and McLain (Commander of XIX Corps). The generals met there with the commanding officers of artillery and infantry units who would make the initial Roer crossing.[128] Bradley recalled in his memoirs that, "We were immensely impressed . . . with the planning" for Grenade.[129] The attack was to begin on February 23.

On February 18, my father told his parents that he had sent them a souvenir from the submarine pens at Brest (a clock) and a copy of the "Division History, in more or less picture form." He described the history as "very interesting indeed," and noted that it "will serve as an excellent guide to relate stories once this war is over." In this letter, my father's thoughts, as they often did, turned to the well-being of his parents. "If there is anything I can do to help out matters at home, financially or otherwise," he wrote, "let me know."

Preparations for the offensive continued right up to February 22. The After Action Report details these preparations. The 30th Division would attack on the left and the 29th Division, led by my father's regiment, would lead the way, supported by tank battalions, tank-destroyer battalions, and a chemical mortar battalion.[130]

Two attacking battalions assembled in forward areas at approximately 7:00pm on February 22. Their initial task was to cross the river and provide cover to engineers who would construct the foot bridges and infantry support bridges, then move forward south of Julich and seize initial objectives while protecting the right flank of the division.[131]

The 116th regiment was ordered to assemble in forward areas early on February 23 to cross the river in the 175th's zone. The 121st Engineer Combat battalion was tasked with crossing the 115th regiment using "assault boats." The battalion was also in charge of constructing the foot bridges and infantry support bridges. When the enemy was cleared from the east bank of the Roer, the 121st Engineers were to "construct a treadway and a pontoon bridge" and assemble, construct, and operate a "ferry service."[132]

On the eve of this great offensive, my father simply noted in a letter: "Have been busy all morning and shall be likewise this afternoon."

February 22 witnessed a "day-long air attack" on enemy positions on the east bank of the Roer as well as rear supply positions between Duren and Cologne.[133] At approximately 2:45am on February 23, division, corps, and army artillery "lit up the whole of the river's east bank."[134] The east bank of the Roer and areas beyond were pounded by intense shelling joined by mortar, tank, and machine gun fire. Joseph Ewing described it as "a great destructive bludgeon which was hammering all life and resistance out of Julich . . . and the east bank."[135] The artillery, writes Charles MacDonald, "thundered Armageddon, illuminating the night . . . ."[136] The artillery barrage continued without letup for nearly an hour, streaking and bursting flashes of light that illuminated the wrecked buildings of Julich.[137]

At about 3:00am, two companies of my father's regiment crossed the Roer in assault boats and occupied positions along the east bank where they could provide cover for the engineers.[138] At 3:30am, the engineers began constructing the bridges and came under enemy light artillery fire.[139] One foot bridge was disabled when an assault boat carried by the swift current of the still-flooded river accidentally struck it. "[A]lmost everywhere," historian Russell Weigley noted, "the still-flooded river, abetted by German artillery fire, played havoc with bridgebuilding."[140] As soon as the bridges were built, the infantry poured across.[141] The sturdier pontoon bridge was not in place until nearly 4:45am.[142]

The 175th's 1st battalion crossed the Roer on foot bridges and moved toward the center of Julich. The 2nd battalion crossed next and moved to an area north of the Citadel. At about 7:15am, my father and his battalion crossed the river.[143] Throughout the day, German rocket, mortar and artillery fire harassed the bridge sites and inflicted casualties among the Americans.[144]

Initially, enemy resistance was moderate to light, but as the attack over the river progressed enemy resistance stiffened.[145] Weigley notes that "the assault crossing of the Roer proved . . . the most difficult phase of Operation Grenade."[146]

My father's February 23 letter to his parents stated simply, but ominously, "Am plenty busy today so this letter will be brief."

The second day's attack by the 29th Division began at 8:00am and was again led by my father's regiment and the 115th. My father's battalion moved south, securing a factory and other locations on the southern edge of Julich. Meanwhile, the 175th's 1st battalion advanced along the Julich-Cologne highway, seized Setternich, and linked-up with units of the 30th Division. The 2nd battalion attacked northeast of Julich near Merscherhue and Neuhaus. The Citadel fell that day to a company of the 116th regiment and the 739th tank battalion.[147] Julich was now in American hands.

My father's February 24 letter to his parents again mentioned that he was "being kept plenty busy."

The 29th Division small newspaper, 29 Let's Go, noted in its February 25 issue that the Ninth and First Armies "are across the Roer River." "Julich has been taken," the paper noted, "and there's fighting in Duren." The paper reported that General Eisenhower "said that the offensive should mark the beginning of the destruction of the German forces west of the Rhine."

Another story in the paper told about the division's capture of Julich. "The long-awaited offensive," the paper noted, "which started . . . with one of the most astonishing artillery barrages of the war, found the 175th on the west side of the Roer ready and raring to go." The story praised the work of the combat engineers in "erecting the footbridges across the fast-flowing river and in ferrying troops . . . in assault crafts under artillery and small arms fire." The story concluded by noting that troops of the 175th raised a banner "across the gothic gateway to the historic fortress town." The banner read: "This is Julich, Germany. Sorry its so messed up. But we were in a hurry--29th (Blue & Gray) Division."[148]

On February 25, after a brief period of rest and reorganization, my father's regiment joined with the rest of the division and the entire Ninth Army in a swing to the northeast toward Munchen-Gladbach and Dusseldorf. Ewing described this as "a giant flanking movement that was designed to strike the enemy across his lines of communication."[149] For this advance, the 175th's 1st battalion assembled in Mersch, the 2nd battalion moved to Gevelsdorf, and my father's battalion assembled in Hasselsweiler. The 1st battalion was on the left, my father's was in the center, and the 2nd battalion was on the right. The After Action Report notes that "the advance was rapid throughout the day."[150]

My father's battalion advanced from Beverath to Kockum to Keyenberg to Borschemich.[151]

On February 28, the whole division continued to advance rapidly. My father's regiment that day took Wanlo, Wickrathberg, Gudderath, then Odenkirchen.[152]

My father was now on the outskirts of Munchen-Gladbach, a large industrial city. The first phase of Operation Grenade had succeeded in crossing the Roer, seizing Julich, and moving northeast in its drive to link-up with the Canadians at Wesel. The Ninth Army, including my father's division, had done its job well.

General Bradley later wrote that the Ninth Army's attack across the Roer toward the Rhine "was one of the most perfectly executed of the war. In a mere two weeks the Ninth Army drove about fifty-three miles from the Roer to the Rhine . . . ." He noted further that the attack "cleared thirty-four miles of the west bank of the Rhine . . . capturing some 30,000 German troops." Bradley also noted that the offensive "unhinged German defenses in front of [the Canadian Army], enabling the [British and Canadians] to drive forward another twenty-three miles to link up" with the Ninth Army at Wesel, "capturing another 22,000 German troops."[153]

MUNCHEN-GLADBACH AND ACROSS THE RHINE

On March 1, 1945, my father's regiment was poised to move into Munchen-Gladbach from a line stretching from Gudderath to Geistenbeck. The 116th regiment was on the right near Durselen and Watt, while the 115th was in division reserve near Jackerath, Titz, and Opherten. The 747th Tank battalion's companies were variously attached to all three infantry regiments of the division.[154]

At 7:00am, the 175th and 116th regiments attacked toward the city. Munchen-Gladbach was the first large city in Germany encountered by the 29th Division. Joseph Ewing described it as a "great sprawling city of factories and gray stone buildings." It was home to cotton, silk, wool, and iron industries.[155] The 116th moved on the right, bypassing the center of the city, while my father's regiment pushed through Rheydt and into the streets of Munchen-Gladbach.[156] Both regiments met "light to moderate resistance" from rifle, anti-tank, anti-aircraft and self-propelled-gun fire.[157]

By day's end, the 116th effectively cleared Korschenbroich, Herrenshoff, Neersbroich, Geisenkirchen, and Baueshuette.[158]

The big story that day, however, was the capture of Munchen-Gladbach by my father's regiment. This was the largest German city to fall to the Allies as of that date in the war.

On March 2, my father's regiment occupied the northwest section of the city. "No quarters occupied by the Division in Europe up to that time," wrote Joseph Ewing, "had ever been so sumptuous."[159] The tired soldiers, my father included, now lived and slept in undamaged apartments with running water, electric lights, and soft beds.[160] Beer was plentiful for a while, and the soldiers even located some champagne.[161]

My father wrote to his parents on March 2, after being on the attack for 10 days. "Haven't had the opportunity of writing during the past several days," he noted. "Guess the [news]papers told you what is going on. No need for me to go into detail."

On March 3, the exhausted 29th Division was placed in Ninth Army reserve and removed from XIX Corps. That day, my father mentioned in a letter that he had "some good champagne yesterday."

The soldiers of the 29th Division underwent physical and dental examinations on March 4. The men also received training and instructions on issues of looting, range firing, fraternization, small unit tactics, road marches, and after combat discussions. Trainers and instructors pointed out combat mistakes and emphasized the valuable lessons learned from such mistakes.[162] That same day, my father responded to news that two more soldiers he knew from back home had been killed in battle. "Such are the fortunes of war," he wrote.

The 29th Division stayed in Munchen-Gladbach for about one week. The city soon became a rear area headquarters for armies advancing toward the Rhine.[163] My father's regiment moved out of the city to Wickrathberg on March 11.[164]

On March 7, my father told his parents in a letter that he received their package containing peanuts, fruit cake, and handkerchiefs. He asked them, "Is there anything I can do for you . . . If there is just let me know." He also advised them not to get their hopes up about him coming home anytime soon. "Don't expect me home until this mess is over, over here."

On March 9, 1945, my father was awarded the Bronze Star. The citation accompanying the medal reads as follows:

> T Sgt Frank F. Sempa, 33024465 (then S Sgt and T Sgt), 175th, US Army, for meritorious service in military operations against the enemy in Western Europe. From 7 June 1944 to 13 February 1945, T Sgt Sempa, Communications Sergeant, excelled in the performance of his duties and contributed materially to the fine record established by the organization of which he is a member. The high standards of courage, initiative and discipline required during long periods of combat were met by T Sgt Sempa in a manner that reflect great credit upon himself and the Military Service. Entered Military Service from Pennsylvania.

In his March 9 letter to his parents, he informed them simply that he "Got a Bronze Star today."

The division's regiments continued to train, receiving instructions and critiques from intelligence and reconnaissance units. Equipment was inspected. Soldiers were tested regarding their knowledge and understanding of vehicles, demolitions, field orders, range estimations, communications, map reading, first aid, patrolling, scouting, aggressive reconnaissance, minefields, crossing streams and rivers, flank protection, road blocks, and anti-tank ditches.[165]

My father mentioned in his March 13 letter, one of the new luxuries of rear area life. "Just finished taking a bath, one of those you take in a tub," he wrote. "Felt just like my baby days."

On March 17, my father's battalion assumed guard duty at Ninth Army head-quarters, relieving a battalion of the 115th regiment. It performed that duty until it was relieved by the 116th's 1st battalion on March 24.[166]

My father mentioned in a St. Patrick's Day letter to his parents that "a lot of our boys are going back to England to get married." He predicted that "There's going to be plenty of English gals going back to the USA after this war is over."

On March 19, my father sent a $50 money order home so his mother could buy a new coat. He also sent home another souvenir that he described in a letter. It was a "large Nazi flag" that "flew over a large German garrison until we took it over."

Training for my father's regiment continued throughout March. Past combat operations were analyzed with the goal of correcting any deficiencies noted in past operations. The regiment also prepared for future combat with all units practicing operations "in fast moving situations."[167]

Communications soldiers, including my father, participated in training and in-struction on the use of radios in fast moving operations. Engineers studied and practiced demolitions and the reduction of obstacles. Artillery units tested the firing of their weapons.[168]

Battalions in each of the division's infantry regiments prepared field exercises to demonstrate proficiency in assembly and movement on roads; changing direc-tion while marching on a broad front; use of flank guards and covering force; rapid and wide maneuver; attacking enemy armor and self-propelled guns in towns; and advancing in coordination with tanks.[169]

The weather in late March took a turn for the better, and my father noted that fact plus the beneficial effect of good weather on the war effort. In two letters written on March 23, my father wrote, "Spring weather is treating us royally. Its ideal flying weather and Jerry is catching merry hell." "The air corps," he noted, "calls it 'Victory Weather.' Hope they're correct." Two days later, my father wrote, "Our spring weather remains just what you would want it to be. Hope it stays that way. It gives the air corps time to work on those bums." Again, on March 28: "Our Spring weather continues ideal. Hope it stays that way. Its ideal flying weather and should shorten this war over here."

Since January, Allied air forces had escalated the strategic bombing of Ger-man cities by day and night. In 1945, allied air forces dropped more than 1.18 million tons of bombs on Dusseldorf, Cologne, Dresden, Hamburg, Berlin, Bremen, Duinsberg, Frankfurt, Essen, Munich, Hanover, Nuremberg, Stuttgart, Mannheim, and other cities.[170] More than a half-million German homes were de-stroyed in bombing raids. More than seven million people were rendered home-less. Approximately 600,000 Germans died as a result of the bombing cam-paign.[171]

Max Hastings points out that the Allied strategic bombing campaign "was a military operation designed to hasten the collapse of Germany's ability to make war. It stopped as soon as Hitler's people ceased to fight." The bombing pro-duced militarily significant results. In 1945, Hastings notes, German industrial production "declined relentlessly."[172] The view from the infantry soldier was

simple, as reflected in my father's letters. The bombing of Germany would hopefully shorten the war.

Ending the war and getting home was on every American soldiers' mind. In
my father's March 25 letter, he informed his parents that "Stars and Stripes . . .
announced the plan for discharging men after Victory in Europe, would be com-
pleted shortly but would not be announced until after Germany is defeated." He
then explained the factors to be considered in which soldiers would be sent
home first: "Total length of service, time overseas, combat time, decorations,
and dependents." "At that rate," he noted, "I should stand a . . . chance, I hope."
He wrote that he was not "worrying about it until the last shot is fired over here."

Early in March, the First U.S. Army crossed the Rhine River, after seizing intact the Ludendorff Bridge at Remagen.[173] Patton's Third Army crossed the river
on March 22. The next day, the Canadian First Army, British Second Army, and
the U.S. Ninth Army crossed the mighty river.[174]

On March 31 and April 1, my father's division crossed the Rhine north of
Rheinberg.[175] On April 1, my father wished his parents a Happy Easter and mentioned that he was "being kept plenty busy."

In early April, the 29th Division, except for the 116th regiment, was in XVI
Corps reserve where it trained and conducted reconnaissance missions along the
Rhein-Herne Canal and the Lippe River. The 116th regiment was temporarily attached to the 75th Division for operations north of the Ruhr pocket.[176] On April
3, the division assumed responsibility for protecting the Lippe River bridges.

On April 5, my father reminded his parents in a letter that he was "celebrating
an anniversary today, 30 months overseas. Seems like a mighty long time."

Beginning in the second week of April, the 29th Division was assigned the
task of controlling "Displaced Persons" and Allied Prisoners of War (POWs) in
the division's sector. Each regiment was responsible for a specific geographical
area.[177] The division's troops also provided security for the Ninth Army's rear
area.[178] That assignment continued until April 18.

On April 10, my father wrote that he has "been kept busy during the past several days." He also mentioned that the weather continued to be good. "Ideal flying weather," he wrote, "and the air corps sure is laying it on. The more the mer-
rier. It should get us home that much sooner."

Two days later, my father wrote: "War news sure is looking good and it may
not be too long."

On April 12, 1945, President Roosevelt died after suffering a massive stroke in
Warm Springs, Georgia. The news of the Commander-in-Chief's death quickly
spread to the troops. The next day, my father wrote to his parents: "News of
FDR's death came as a distinct shock to all of us here. Its a shame he didn't live
to see the victory he fought so hard for."

Three days later, news spread among the troops about the Russian offensive
toward Berlin. My father wrote that day that he "just heard the war news and it
reports that the Russians have launched their long awaited Berlin drive."

During April 9 to April 18, the 29th Division controlled 146 Displaced Person
Camps, holding more than 72,000 Displaced Persons, and 89 POW camps with

more than 40,000 POWs.[179]

The division was transferred from Ninth Army reserve to XVI Corps on April 12.[180] On April 19, my father's regiment was relieved of its Displaced Person and POW duties by units of the 95th Infantry and XVI Corps' artillery soldiers.[181]

Ninth Army Commander General William Simpson officially commended the 29th Division for its tactical combat role in his army and its performance of the "extremely difficult and complicated task" of providing security for the rear area and managing the Displaced Persons and POWs.[182]

By April 19, 1945, other Ninth Army units and the British Second Army had rapidly advanced to the Elbe River, some 300 miles from Berlin. The rapid advance had resulted in an 18-mile by 35-mile area where enemy troops had not been cleared.[183]

The 29th Division was ordered to join XIII Corps and assigned to clear enemy troops from the area bypassed by the American and British armies on their way to the Elbe. My father's regiment moved to a forward assembly area for this assignment on April 20, along with attached mortar and medical support units.[184] The next day, the 175th began clearing out several wooded areas near the city of Klotze, where enemy forces had ambushed Allied supply columns.[185] This combat action continued through April 25, resulting in the capture of more than 130 enemy prisoners. More than 45 of the enemy were killed.[186] My father later recalled that, "Our regiment was assigned to clear pockets of resistance and [take] up defensive positions along the west bank of the Elbe River."[187]

On April 22, the day that his battalion cleared a wooded area north of Klotze, my father wrote two letters. He told his parents that he had "been very busy the last few days." He also informed them that he turned down an appointment as a warrant officer because it would have meant "leaving the outfit." He confidently predicted that the "war over here will soon be over."

In his second letter that day (to his brother Johnnie), my father wrote: "Being kept plenty busy . . . Won't be very much longer and this mess over here will be finished." He also told his brother that he "turned down an appointment as a warrant officer." "It meant leaving the outfit I am now in," he explained, "so I said no . . . Been in this outfit over four years and don't want to leave it now."

My father also wrote two letters on April 24. In the first one he noted that "It was four years ago today I first had on an army uniform. Time sure is passing." He noted further that, "If at that time anyone had told me I'd be in the army at least four years I'd [have] . . . called them crazy."

In his second letter that day, my father mentioned that, "The Russians sure are going to town," in their drive to Berlin. "I'm going to renew acquaintances with all my Russian friends once I get back," he wrote.

On April 26, my father's regiment and the rest of the 29th Division arrived at the west bank of the Elbe River.[188] The division's river line stretched for nearly 40 miles in the center between the British 5th Division on the left and the U.S. 84th division on the right.[189]

On April 27, my father informed his parents that he was "busy the last few days." "War news is good," he wrote. "Shouldn't be too long before this mess is over." The next day, he wrote: "War news is excellent. The end over here shouldn't be too far away and then maybe I'll get a chance to get home." "I've seen enough of the world," he continued, "and I'm ready to settle down."

My father's April 29 letter revealed that the war was winding down. He mentioned eating pork chops, pickled beets, bread and butter, and raisin pudding for supper, playing volleyball, and having fresh eggs for breakfast.

The After Action Report notes that at the end of April, the 29th Division occupied a portion of the Elbe River line with four battalions. The other battalions were tasked with "Military Government duties," including control of Displaced Persons and Allied prisoners of war, and the evacuation of civilians behind the front line.[190]

Joseph Ewing noted that at the end of April the front line at the Elbe witnessed "hardly a sight or sound of war." The enemy was on the other side of the river awaiting the impending arrival of the Red Army. On April 30, three German officers crossed the Elbe hoisting a white flag. They offered to surrender an entire ten-thousand man V-2 Rocket division before the Russians arrived.[191]

VICTORY IN EUROPE

General Eisenhower's decision to halt U.S. and Allied forces at the Elbe River in the Spring of 1945, instead of advancing toward Berlin, produced controversy at the time and ever since. It was a decision, however, that fully complied with the general outline of President Roosevelt's policy to get along with our Russian allies at the end of the war. Indeed, Robert Nisbet insightfully referred to FDR's approach to Stalin toward the end of the war as "the failed courtship."[192]

When Eisenhower in late March cabled Stalin to inform him of American and British intentions to leave the taking of Berlin to the Red Army, Churchill telephoned the supreme commander to urge an "advance as far eastward as possible."[193]

In his history of the Second World War, Churchill reflected on the grave political consequences that flowed from Eisenhower's military decision. "The indispensable political direction," he wrote, "was lacking at the moment it was most needed. The United States stood on the scene of victory, master of world fortunes, but without a true and coherent design."[194]

Eisenhower defended his decision to the Combined Chiefs of Staff, reasoning that "Berlin has lost much of its former military importance."[195] Both Bradley and Marshall sided with Eisenhower.[196]

In an interview published in the *Scranton Tribune* after the war, my father observed that American forces "would have been to Berlin in a few days but the agreement . . . was for the Russians to make that capture."[197]

On May 1, the 116th and 175th regiments, including my father's battalion, occupied the front line on the west bank of the Elbe.[198] During the next two days, nearly ten thousand Germans comprising an entire V-2 Rocket Division crossed the river to surrender to the 29th in order to avoid a far worse fate at the hands of the Red Army.[199]

On May 2, a five man patrol from my father's battalion crossed the Elbe and made contact with Russian soldiers.[200]

While all of this was going on at the Elbe, my father informed his parents on May 1 that he "wouldn't be surprised to see this war over here. . . over by the time this letter reaches you. Things are happening fast . . . ." Things, indeed, were happening fast. Hitler had committed suicide in his bunker in Berlin. German forces were surrendering in large numbers.

The soldiers of the 29th Division were initially notified in early May that they were being moved from XIII Corps to XVI Corps and would resume Military Government duties in the vicinity of Schwalenberg, Steinkenn, and Guterslor. This order was quickly changed and the division instead was assigned to the Munster area, with division headquarters at Warendorf, the 115th regiment north of Warendorf, the 116th at Isselhorst, and my father's regiment at Beelen.[201]

My father's division was designated "Task Force Bremen," and its area of control included the ports of Bremen and Bremerhaven. These ports were to be used as "the supply ports for all United States Occupational forces." Working in conjunction with Allied naval units, the division was responsible for "storage and disposal of enemy war material," control of factories, disarming the enemy fleet, guarding naval installations, and operating port facilities. The infantry units also provided security for the area.[202]

As my father's division moved westward on May 4, the radio announced the surrender of large numbers of German forces in the northwest. "Just heard the good news of Germany surrendering in Northern Germany, Denmark, etc," my father informed his parents in a May 4 letter. "It should all be over any time now."

The next day, my father wrote, "Guess you know as much about the war news as I do. It seems to be all over . . .over here, but the final details have yet to come . . . ." In this letter, my father also mentioned that he had seen a German slave labor camp. "Everything you read about those German camps is true," he wrote. "I saw one of them and let me tell you it was brutal." "You should [have] seen this camp," he continued. "Very very brutal. Can't understand how anybody could treat people like the Germans treated the slave laborers."

My father did not mention the name or location of the camp he saw, but the United States Holocaust Memorial Museum's website credits the 29th Division for liberating the Dinslaken civilian slave labor camp in April 1945.[203] Most likely, this was the camp my father mentioned in his letter. On May 6, my father wrote, "Guess you're aware that everything is almost over . . . over here. Hope that means going home for us old timers."

On May 7, my father shared the joyous news that the war was over and Victory in Europe Day would be declared the next day. "The radio just informed us," he wrote, "that tomorrow, 8 May, will be V-E Day. That's the day we have all been waiting for!" He explained that, "Here, we have been aware all day long that the big show over here is all over." "Guess the celebrations back home were on a grand scale," he continued. "Guess I'll go and get drunk tomorrow. It sure is worth a celebration. It sure has been a long and hard struggle."

The next day, the 29th Division's small newspaper, *29 Let's Go*, published a special "Victory Issue" entitled "D-Day to V-E Day." "Today," the paper noted, "is Victory-In-Europe Day!" The story noted that British Prime Minister Churchill will broadcast at 1500 hours, to be followed by the King of England. The paper noted that the King sent congratulations to General Eisenhower "on the success of the Allied Armies."[204]

The surrender, the paper reported, occurred at 0241 hours on May 7. General Jodl, the German Chief of Staff, signed the surrender documents.

"For the men of the Blue and Gray," the paper noted, "V-E Day was an anticlimax, coming as it did on D-plus-336."[205]

The paper included an outline, noting the key dates and events, of the 29th Division's, and my father's, journey from Omaha Beach to the Elbe River. It concluded with a message from the division commander, General Gerhardt: "Omaha Beach to the Elbe River--Isigny, St. Lo, Vire, Brest, Siegfried Line, Roer River--objectives taken on the way." "We trained hard," Gerhardt noted, "for a difficult task, have high standards and a record of all missions accomplished. Our success is a direct result of the efforts of all individuals throughout."[206]

The "Victory Issue" did not neglect the division's comrades in arms still fighting in the Pacific theater. "American Super-Fortresses have made their eighteenth attack on Kyushu, the southern island of Japan," it noted. "American carrier planes have again attacked airfields on an island off Okinawa." The paper also mentioned that Allied warplanes were operating from airfields captured by Australian troops in Borneo.[207]

The After Action Report notes that Victory in Europe was celebrated by all units of the 29th Division. There were parades and memorial ceremonies.[208] On May 9, my father wrote that he "attended a Memorial Service today for those who had died in battle." He also mentioned that, "With the war now over we are anxiously awaiting word on what they intend to do with us." He expressed the hope that "something good is in store for us."

The next day, my father noted in a letter that the weather was very hot. "Right now," he wrote, "I could stand a half dozen bottles of cold beer."

On May 11, my father informed his parents that the army announced the "Demobilization Point System." "I have the necessary points," he explained, "but that's as far as I'm going to commit myself." He promised he would keep them "posted on developments. If everything goes as planned . . . who knows but that I might be home before the year is out."

The After Action Report notes that beginning on May 11, the soldiers of the 29th were shown the film "Two down and One To Go," to remind them that their fellow soldiers were still fighting and dying in the Pacific.[209] The film also hinted that redeployment to the Pacific was a real possibility for those in the division who did not have the necessary "points."[210]

Joseph Ewing noted that the "point" system was part of every soldier's daily conversation. The system assigned "points" for "length of service, marital status, and battle credits."[211]

A soldier needed 84 points to begin his journey home. My father had 105 points. On May 21, my father again noted in a letter that he had "the necessary points" to be discharged. "Now all they have to do is declare me non-essential. I'm keeping my fingers crossed." In that letter, my father also informed his parents that he was stationed "near the port of Bremen."

The next day he wrote that "Going HOME" is the topic of conversation among the troops. On a lighter note, he mentioned that "six girls write to me steadily and each of them [has] the same idea in mind . . . marriage." He estimated that it would probably take months to get home even though he had enough "points."

He also recalled in that letter a time "when the going was rough." "I remember one instance in particular," he wrote, "when the Germans bombed and strafed us continuously for over an hour." "I happened to be out of my cellar at that time," he explained, "and was even caught without a helmet. God was with me that day."

On May 25, 1945, my father was promoted to Master Sergeant. In a letter written that day, he informed his parents of the promotion and noted that he was getting "plenty of sleep these nights. No interruptions since the war ended."

Two days later, my father informed his parents that he thought he had 105 points, which was enough to be sent home. On May 29, he again mentioned that "I do have enough points. In fact I have some to spare. If we get another combat (Battle) Star I should have 105 points. Now all they have to do is send me home and declare me non-essential." Again on May 30, my father wrote, "Nothing new on getting home . . . Hope it won't be too long."

On May 30, the division held ceremonies paying tribute to those who had died in battle from Omaha Beach to the Elbe. Without such men, the After Action Report noted, "victory would have been impossible." That same day in Holland, General Gerhardt placed a wreath on the grave of a 29th Division soldier.[212]

"The war in Europe had ended for the 29th Division," notes the After Action Report. It was "a war for which the Division had trained since 3 February 1941." From D-Day to V-E Day, "a series of long, hard struggles through Normandy, Brest, Holland, and finally Germany had been waged with victory always close, but still out of reach." "Finally," the Report notes, "[the end] had come."[213]

NOTES

1. For a discussion of Bullitt's efforts to persuade FDR to adopt a more political approach to the war, see Francis P. Sempa, "William C. Bullitt: Diplomat and Prophet," in the Introduction to William Bullitt, *The Great Globe Itself: A Preface to World Affairs* (New Brunswick, NJ: Transaction Publishers 2005), pp. vii-xlix.

2. Bradley, *A General's Life*, p. 333.

3. H. Essame, *Patton: A Study in Command* (New York: Charles Scribner's Sons 1974), p. 202.

ing Germany 77

4. Max Hastings, *Armageddon: The Battle for Germany, 1944-1945* (New York: Alfred A. Knopf 2004), p. 62.

5. John Ellis, *Brute Force: Allied Strategy and Tactics in the Second World War* (New York: Viking 1990), p. 420.

6. B. H. Liddell Hart, *History of the Second World War* (New York: A Perigee Book 1982), pp. 561-562.

7. Stephen Ambrose, *The Supreme Commander: The War Years of General Dwight D. Eisenhower* (Garden City, NY: Doubleday & Company, Inc. 1969), pp. 527-535.

8. Churchill, *Triumph and Tragedy*, p. 157.

9. Hastings, *Armageddon*, p. 72.

10. Charles B. MacDonald, *The Mighty Endeavor: The American War in Europe* (New York: Da Capo 1992), pp. 384-385.

11. Ewing, *29 Let's Go*, p. 149.

12. Ewing, *29 Let's Go*, p. 150.

13. "D-Day to V-E Day," *29 Let's Go*, May 8, 1945. This was a small division newspaper that reported on the 29th Division's progress, the other war news, and stories about people and events in the United States. This particular issue was published on V-E Day and noted key dates and events in the division's progress from Omaha Beach to the end of the war.

14. Charles B. MacDonald, *The Siegfried Line Campaign* (Washington, D.C: Center of Military History 1990), p. 35; www.history.army.mil/books/wwii/Siegfried/Siegfried Line/siegfried.htm.

15. "Breaching the Siegfried Line," XIX Corps General Staff analysis, www.xixcorps.nl/Breaching_the_Siegfried_Line.htm

16. Charles B. MacDonald, *The Mighty Endeavor: The American War in Europe* (New York: Da Capo Press 1992), p. 363.

17. MacDonald, *The Siegfried Line Campaign*, p. 402.

18. "Breaching the Siegfried Line."

19. Ewing, *29 Let's Go*, p. 151.

20. "XIX Corps Combat Chronology," October 1944, www.xixcorps.nl/XIX_Corps_Chronology_October_1944.htm.

21. Ewing, *29 Let's Go*, p. 154.

22. *After Action Report*, 115th Infantry, 29th Division, October 1944.

23. "XIX Corps Combat Chronology," October 1944.

24. Ewing, *29 Let's Go*, p. 158.

25. Ewing, *29 Let's Go*, p. 159.

26. Ewing, *29 Let's Go*, p. 161.

27. Memo from Lt. Col. William C. Purnell to Commanding General, 29th Division, 7 October 1944. I found a copy of this memo min my father's scrapbook.

28. *After Action Report*, 115th Infantry, 29th Division, October 1944.

29. Ewing, *29 Let's Go*, p. 163.

30. *29 Let's Go, WWII GI Stories*, www.lonesentry.com/gi_stories_booklets/29th Infantry/

31. *After Action Report*, 115th Infantry, 29th Division, October 1944.

32. MacDonald, *The Siegfried Line Campaign*, p. 391.

33. MacDonald, *The Siegfried Line Campaign*, p. 400.

34. *After Action Report*, 29th Division, November 1944.

35. Ewing, *29 Let's Go*, p. 169.

36. *After Action Report*, 29th Division, November 1944.

37. *After Action Report*, 29th Division, November 1944.

38. Ewing, *29 Let's Go*, p. 169.
39. Ewing, *29 Let's Go*, p. 169.
40. *After Action Report*, 29th Division, November 1944.
41. Ewing, *29 Let's Go*, p. 169.
42. *After Action Report*, 29th Division, November 1944; Ewing, *29 Let's Go*, p. 170-171.
43. MacDonald, *The Mighty Endeavor*, p. 384.
44. MacDonald, *The Siegfried Line Campaign*, pp. 497, 524.
45. Weigley, *Eisenhower's Lieutenants*, pp. 618-619.
46. Weigley, *Eisenhower's Lieutenants*, p. 621.
47. MacDonald, *The Siegfried Line Campaign*, p. 519; Weigley, *Eisenhower's Lieutenants*, p. 621.
48. *After Action Report*, 29th Division, November 1944.
49. Weigley, *Eisenhower's Lieutenants*, p. 621.
50. Ewing, *29 Let's Go*, p. 170.
51. Weigley, *Eisenhower's Lieutenants*, p. 621.
52. Weigley, *Eisenhower's Lieutenants*, p. 623.
53. *After Action Report*, 29th Division, November 1944.
54. Ewing, *29 Let's Go*, p. 175.
55. Ewing, *29 Let's Go*, p. 175.
56. *After Action Report*, 29th Division, November 1944.
57. MacDonald, *The Siegfried Line Campaign*, p. 538; *After Action Report*, 29th Division, November 1944.
58. *After Action Report*, 29th Division, November 1944.
59. *After Action Report*, 29th Division, November 1944.
60. Ewing, *29 Let's Go*, p. 181.
61. *After Action Report*, 29th Division, November 1944; Ewing, *29 Let's Go*, p. 181.
62. *After Action Report*, 29th Division, November 1944; Ewing, *29 Let's Go*, p. 194.
63. *After Action Report*, 29th Division, November 1944.
64. *After Action Report*, 29th Division, November 1944.
65. *After Action Report*, 29th Division, November 1944.
66. *After Action Report*, 29th Division, November 1944.
67. Ewing, *29 Let's Go*, p. 186.
68. Ewing, *29 Let's Go*, p. 186-187.
69. *After Action Report*, 29th Division, November 1944.
70. *After Action Report*, 29th Division, November 1944; Ewing, *29 Let's Go*, p. 187.
71. *After Action Report*, 29th Division, November 1944; Ewing, *29 Let's Go*, p. 187.
72. *After Action Report*, 29th Division, November 1944.
73. *After Action Report*, 29th Division, November 1944.
74. Ewing, *29 Let's Go*, p. 187.
75. MacDonald, *The Siegfried Line Campaign*, p. 561.
76. *After Action Report*, 29th Division, November 1944.
77. *After Action Report*, 29th Division, November 1944.
78. Ewing, *29 Let's Go*, p. 304.
79. Ewing, *29 Let's Go*, pp. 193-198.
80. *After Action Report*, 29th Division, December 1944.
81. Bradley, *A General's Life*, p. 343.
82. Hastings, *Armageddon*, p. 66-67.
83. Weigley, *Eisenhower's Lieutenants*, p. 635.
84. Hastings, *Armageddon*, p. 189.

85. *After Action Report*, 29th Division, December 1944; Ewing, *29 Let's Go*, p. 201.

86. *After Action Report*, 29th Division, December 1944.

87. *After Action Report*, 29th Division, December 1944.

88. *After Action Report*, 29th Division, December 1944.

89. Ewing, *29 Let's Go*, p. 203.

90. *After Action Report*, 29th Division, December 1944.

91. *After Action Report*, 29th Division, January 1945.

92. *After Action Report*, 29th Division, January 1945.

93. *After Action Report*, 29th Division, January 1945.

94. *After Action Report*, 29th Division, January 1945.

95. Ewing, *29 Let's Go*, p. 211.

96. Ewing, *29 Let's Go*, p. 213.

97. *After Action Report*, 29th Division, January 1945.

98. Ewing, *29 Let's Go*, p. 211.

99. *After Action Report*, 29th Division, January 1945; Ewing, *29 Let's Go*, p. 213.

100. *After Action Report*, 29th Division, January 1945.

101. *After Action Report*, 29th Division, January 1945.

102. Ewing, *29 Let's Go*, p. 216.

103. Charles Whiting, *West Wall: The Battle for Hitler's Siegfried Line, September 1944-March 1945* (London: Pan Books 2002), p. 51.

104. Ewing, *29 Let's Go*, p. 216.

105. Hastings, *Armageddon*, p. 246-247.

106. Ewing, *29 Let's Go*, p. 216.

107. *After Action Report*, 29th Division, January 1945.

108. Hastings, *Armageddon*, p. 235.

109. Weigley, *Eisenhower's Lieutenants*, p. 839.

110. Weigley, *Eisenhower's Lieutenants*, p. 841.

111. Churchill, *Triumph and Tragedy*, pp. 403-404.

112. Churchill, *Triumph and Tragedy*, p. 404.

113. Bradley, *A General's Life*, p. 391.

114. Hastings, *Armageddon*, p. 339.

115. MacDonald, *The Mighty Endeavor*, p. 465.

116. Ambrose, *The Supreme Commander*, p. 612.

117. *After Action Report*, 29th Division, February 1945.

118. *After Action Report*, 29th Division, February 1945.

119. *After Action Report*, 29th Division, February 1945.

120. *After Action Report*, 29th Division, February 1945.

121. Ewing, *29 Let's Go*, p. 218-219.

122. *After Action Report*, 29th Division, February 1945.

123. Ewing, *29 Let's Go*, p. 219.

124. *After Action Report*, 29th Division, February 1945.

125. Weigley, *Eisenhower's Lieutenants*, p. 876.

126. Weigley, *Eisenhower's Lieutenants*, p. 885.

127. MacDonald, *The Mighty Endeavor*, p. 469.

128. Ewing, *29 Let's Go*, p. 225.

129. Bradley, *A General's Life*, p. 395.

130. *After Action Report*, 29th Division, February 1945.

131. *After Action Report*, 29th Division, February 1945.

132. *After Action Report*, 29th Division, February 1945.

133. Barry Turner, *Countdown to Victory: The Final European Campaigns of World War II* (New York: William Morrow 2004), p. 190.
134. *After Action Report*, 29th Division, February 1945.
135. Ewing, *29 Let's Go*, p. 228.
136. MacDonald, *The Mighty Endeavor*, p. 470.
137. Ewing, *29 Let's Go*, p. 228.
138. Ewing, *29 Let's Go*, p. 228; *After Action Report*, 29th Division, February 1945.
139. *After Action Report*, 29th Division, February 1945.
140. Weigley, *Eisenhower's Lieutenants*, p. 889.
141. *After Action Report*, 29th Division, February 1945.
142. *After Action Report*, 29th Division, February 1945.
143. *After Action Report*, 29th Division, February 1945.
144. Ewing, *29 Let's Go*, p. 231.
145. *After Action Report*, 29th Division, February 1945.
146. Weigley, *Eisenhower's Lieutenants*, pp. 890-891.
147. *After Action Report*, 29th Division, February 1945; Ewing, *29 Let's Go*, p. 233.
148. *29 Let's Go*, February 25, 1945 issue.
149. Ewing, *29 Let's Go*, p. 234.
150. *After Action Report*, 29th Division, February 1945.
151. *After Action Report*, 29th Division, February 1945; Ewing, *29 Let's Go*, p. 236.
152. *After Action Report*, 29th Division, February 1945; Ewing, *29 Let's Go*, p. 242.
153. Bradley, *A General's Life*, p. 399.
154. *After Action Report*, 29th Division, March 1945.
155. Ewing, *29 Let's Go*, p. 243.
156. *After Action Report*, 29th Division, March 1945; Ewing, *29 Let's Go*, p. 242.
157. *After Action Report*, 29th Division, March 1945; Ewing, *29 Let's Go*, p. 242.
158. *After Action Report*, 29th Division, March 1945.
159. Ewing, *29 Let's Go*, p. 243.
160. Ewing, *29 Let's Go*, p. 243.
161. Ewing, *29 Let's Go*, pp. 242-243.
162. *After Action Report*, 29th Division, March 1945.
163. Ewing, *29 Let's Go*, p. 246.
164. *After Action Report*, 29th Division, March 1945.
165. *After Action Report*, 29th Division, March 1945.
166. *After Action Report*, 29th Division, March 1945.
167. *After Action Report*, 29th Division, March 1945.
168. *After Action Report*, 29th Division, March 1945.
169. *After Action Report*, 29th Division, March 1945.
170. Turner, *Countdown to Victory*, p. 141.
171. Turner, *Countdown to Victory*, pp. 146-147.
172. Hastings, *Armageddon*, pp. 306-309.
173. MacDonald, *The Mighty Endeavor*, pp. 482-483.
174. MacDonald, *The Mighty Endeavor*, pp. 494-497.
175. Ewing, *29 Let's Go*, p. 247.
176. *After Action Report*, 29th Division, April 1945.
177. *After Action Report*, 29th Division, April 1945.
178. Ewing, *29 Let's Go*, p. 250.
179. *After Action Report*, 29th Division, April 1945.
180. *After Action Report*, 29th Division, April 1945.
181. *After Action Report*, 29th Division, April 1945.

182. Ewing, *29 Let's Go*, pp. 251-252.

183. Ewing, *29 Let's Go*, p. 253.

184. *After Action Report*, 29th Division, April 1945.

185. *After Action Report*, 29th Division, April 1945; Ewing, *29 Let's Go*, p. 254.

186. *After Action Report*, 29th Division, April 1945.

187. Sempa, *Scranton Tribune*, June 1, 1969.

188. *After Action Report*, 29th Division, April 1945.

189. Ewing, *29 Let's Go*, p. 255.

190. *After Action Report*, 29th Division, April 1945.

191. Ewing, *29 Let's Go*, pp. 256-257.

192. Robert Nisbet, *Roosevelt and Stalin: The Failed Courtship* (Washington, D.C.: Regnery Gateway, 1988).

193. Ambrose, *The Supreme Commander*, p. 637.

194. Churchill, *Triumph and Tragedy*, p. 456.

195. Hastings, *Armageddon*, p. 421.

196. Bradley, *A General's Life*, pp. 416-421.

197. "Ex-Newswriter Battled Way From Normandy Beachhead to Elbe; Gains Discharge on Points," *Scranton Tribune* (July 9, 1945).

198. *After Action Report*, 29th Division, May 1945.

199. *After Action Report*, 29th Division, May 1945.

200. *After Action Report*, 29th Division, May 1945; Ewing, *29 Let's Go*, p. 259.

201. *After Action Report*, 29th Division, May 1945.

202. *After Action Report*, 29th Division, May 1945.

203. www.ushmm.org/lc_4/focus/pdf/infantry_29.pdf.

204. *29 Let's Go*, May 8, 1945.

205. *29 Let's Go*, May 8, 1945.

206. *29 Let's Go*, May 8, 1945.

207. *29 Let's Go*, May 8, 1945.

208. *After Action Report*, 29th Division, May 1945.

209. *After Action Report*, 29th Division, May 1945.

210. Ewing, *29 Let's Go*, pp. 263-264.

211. Ewing, *29 Let's Go*, p. 263.

212. *After Action Report*, 29th Division, May 1945.

213. *After Action Report*, 29th Division, May 1945.

CHAPTER 6

Home

In late May 1945, the 29th Division took full operational control of the Bremen Enclave. The Enclave, some 1500 square miles in north Germany, consisted mostly of small towns and farms. Its major features were two ports, Bremen and Bremerhaven, and the Weser River.[1]

The 29th Division divided the enclave into four sectors. My father's regiment, headquartered at Osterholz-Scharmbeck, occupied the central sector east of the Weser River. The 116th regiment controlled the northern sector. The 115th regiment controlled the southern sector. The 29th Division's artillery unit occupied the sector west of the Weser.[2]

The Bremen Enclave was home to about 8,000 Displaced Persons, mostly Poles, who had been slave laborers. They lived in four camps, and most expressed an unwillingness to return to Soviet-occupied Poland.[3]

My father stayed in the enclave until June 9, when he was transported back to France, the first step on his way home.[4]

My father's letters from the Bremen Enclave reveal that he had little to do there but wait for the official word that he could go home.

On June 1, he informed his parents that he "did nothing today." Two days later, he mentioned that he was "reading and initializing papers." "Nothing new on my returning to the states," he wrote. On June 5, he wrote: "all goes well with

me. Taking life easy. Not doing a darn thing . . . ." He did note that he expected
"to leave . . . shortly and head for home."

In a letter written one year after D-Day, my father reminisced a bit. "Today,"
he wrote, "had a bit of remembering where we were a year ago today! It sure has
been a long year . . . ." He also mentioned that he had "almost everything ready
for my return to the USA. Will be leaving here soon."

On June 10, 1945, my father informed his parents that he was "now in France
on my way home. Can't say as yet when I'll reach there but maybe I'll beat this
letter [home]." The next day he wrote that he had to take "some shots," and
hoped that he had "the opportunity of flying home." "Will be seeing you soon, I
hope."

On June 14, my father wrote that he was "still very anxious to fly home." The
next day: "Still sweating it out here in France." He complained about the army
bureaucracy. "Such red tape I never saw," he noted.

On June 16, my father mentioned in a letter that he hadn't "any idea as to when
I will get out of here. This army red tape is terrific."

Three days later, my father told his parents that he was "finally leaving here
for another stop in our journey home." He mentioned that he was near Metz and
that it "looks very much as though we definitely will fly home."

The final leg of my father's journey home included flights to Marseilles, Ca-
sablanca, the Azores, Bermuda, Miami, and then to Fort Indiantown Gap in
Pennsylvania.[5]

My father was, in his words, "separated from the service" on July 9, 1945.[6] It
had been more than four years since he left home for Fort Meade to begin his
wartime journey. His Army Separation Qualification Record, dated July 9, 1945,
notes that he spent one month as a private in the basic infantry; eight months as
a sergeant telephone operator; one year and one month as a staff sergeant message center chief; and two years and two months as a sergeant communication
chief, finishing as a master sergeant. It further notes that he was responsible for
wire and radio communication and message center function for his infantry regiment, and that he supervised all communication personnel in the regiment. It
also mentions that he requisitioned supplies and trained communication personnel.

My father served overseas for 33 months. He rose to the rank of Master Sergeant, and earned the Bronze Star, the Combat Infantryman's Badge, the Good
Conduct Ribbon, the Arrowhead for the assault on Omaha Beach, five overseas
stripes, and four major engagement stars.

My father considered himself fortunate to have survived the war unscathed.
The campaign in northwest Europe cost more than 109,800 American lives.
More than 356,600 American soldiers were wounded.[7] My father's division suffered 20,324 casualties during the war, including more than 5,000 dead. His regiment suffered 5,776 casualties, including about 1,000 dead.[8] In his copy of Joseph Ewing's history of the 29th Division, my father placed check marks next to
the names of 13 soldiers from the 175th Infantry Regiment who were listed
among the roster of battle dead; presumably friends made and lost during that

terrible war.

My father never considered himself a hero for his wartime service. He was drafted, he had a job to do, and he did it; it was that simple. I recall him saying more than once that most of the war's real heroes never made it back home.

After the war, he rejoined the staff of the *Scranton Tribune*, where he worked as a reporter and later city editor until 1982. Six years later, on November 7, 1988, my father died of a heart attack. He was 72 years old. His wife, my mother, had died of cancer in 1980.

Some writers have called the Second World War the "good war." There is no such thing as a good war. War is sometimes necessary but it is never "good." War is about death and destruction, and World War II was the most deadly and destructive war in history. All attempts to refine war have failed. General Sherman said, "War is cruelty, you cannot refine it." Air Force General Curtis LeMay explained war this way: "You've got to kill people and when you kill enough of them, they stop fighting."

The Second World War was certainly necessary. Germany, Japan, and Italy were aggressive, expansionist, militaristic powers that threatened the global balance of power and U.S. security. The German and Japanese wartime regimes were also evil (as was our wartime ally, Stalin's Soviet Union). The democracies' efforts at appeasement in the 1930s did not work; indeed, they made war more likely. Winston Churchill, the chief critic of appeasement in the 1930s, believed that a firm and unified policy by the democracies could have avoided war. Perhaps.

It is the infantry soldier that knows war at its worst. My father learned about war by landing on blood-soaked Omaha Beach, fighting among hedgerows, clearing the enemy out of bombed-out towns and villages, and overcoming the fortifications of the Siegfried Line. It was hard. It was dirty. It was bloody. It was frightening.

Writing 25 years after D-Day, my father noted that "as long as one lives he cannot forget the scenes . . . on Omaha Beach, the tough and brutal fighting . . . [and] the cunning and sheer guts of our infantrymen." He wrote, "Those of us who came back unscarred have lived down through the years with memories of the terrible things they saw happen." What he remembered most, however, were "deeds of valor, the courage and devotion to duty, [and] the hidden fears of men in combat."[9]

NOTES

1. Ewing, *29 Let's Go*, p. 261.
2. Ewing, *29 Let's Go*, p. 262.
3. Ewing, *29 Let's Go*, p. 271.
4. *Scranton Tribune*, July 9, 1945.
5. *Scranton Tribune*, July 9, 1945.
6. Sempa, *Scranton Tribune*, June 1969.
7. Hastings, *Armageddon*, p. 490.

8. Ewing, *29 Let's Go*, pp. 304-305.
9. Sempa, *Scranton Tribune*, June 1969.

Appendix

The next three pages contain copies of letters that my father wrote home from England, France, and Germany. The first letter is dated October 13, 1942, and it was written shortly after my father arrived in England after his journey across the Atlantic.

The second letter is dated June 13, 1944, and was written six days after my father landed on Omaha Beach in France.

The third letter is dated May 7, 1945, and was written one day before Victory in Europe (V-E) Day.

Oct. 18, 1942

Dear Mom + Dad!

No doubt by this time you have received my telegram informing you of my safe arrival somewhere in England. I enjoyed the trip here very much. It sure was something to look forward to and was uneventful in every way.

The people of England thus far have treated us well. In fact they couldn't have treated us any better under any circumstances. It's great fun exchanging our money for English coin but I'm catching on very fast. The weather here is rather cool. All in all this is beautiful country — nicer than I have ever seen. Being in England gives one a better conception of what these brave people have gone through. Despite all of their hardships they sure do have spirit. In my opinion this war will be of short duration for nothing will stop us once we get started.

I am feeling excellent, never felt better all my life. Please don't worry about me as I am well and taking good care of myself. Remember me to Theresa, Johnie, Joan, Josephine, the kids and Eddie when writing them. I don't know whether or not I will have the chance to write much. How is Dad feeling? I hope much better.

When you get around to it send me some razor blades, candy (such as orange, lemon and other drops) but do not send anything perishable. I haven't received any mail here yet but expect to one of these days. Our mail is censored thus far be it from me write anything for them to censor!

So from somewhere in England my best of everything and lots of love to you and Dad. Take care of yourselves.

Cheerio
Frankie

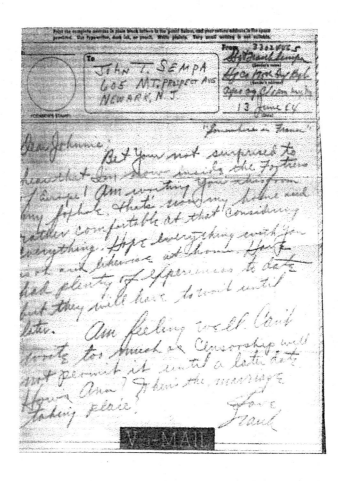

Dear Mom and Dad:

The radio just informed me that tomorrow, May, will be V-E Day. That's the day we've been waiting for! Here, we had been aware, all day long, that the big show over here is all over. Guess the celebrations back home were on a grand scale were they not?

Only mail I got today was a half dozen copies of the Tribune. I finished reading them some time ago and gave them to a guy from Scranton.

Guess I'll go and get drunk tomorrow. It sure is worth a celebration. It sure has been a long and hard struggle.

The news now interesting us is what our status will be? Someday we will get out and others may not. The next few days should tell the tale.

How is Dad feeling? I hope very well.

Nothing else to write about. All goes well with me.

Love

Bibliography

Primary Sources

After Action Reports. 29th Division. June 1944-May 1945. http://www.marylandmilitaryhistory.org/29div/reports/

Memo from Lt. Col. William C. Purnell to Commanding General, 29th Division, 7 October 1944.

Jones, Clifford L., "Neptune: Training, Mounting, the Artificial Ports," Historical Division, U.S. Army Forces, European Theatre, March 1946, www.history.army.mil/documents/wwii/beaches/bchs-7.htm.

"XIX Corps Combat Chronology," October 1944, www.xixcorps.nl/XIX_Corps_Chronology_October_1944.htm.

"Breaching the Siegfried Line," XIX Corps General Staff analysis, www.xixcorps.nl/Breaching_the_Siegfried_Line.htm.

Letters from Frank F. Sempa to Catherine and John Sempa, April 1944 to June 1945. *Frank F. Sempa Papers.* U.S. Army War College. Carlisle, PA.

Books

Ambrose, Stephen E, *The Supreme Commander: The War Years of General Dwight D. Eisenhower.* Garden City, NY: Doubleday & Company, Inc. 1969.

Ambrose, Stephen E, *Citizen Soldiers: The U.S. Army From the Normandy Beaches to the Bulge to the Surrender of Germany.* New York: Touchstone 1997.

Balkoski, Joseph, *Beyond the Beachhead: The 29th Infantry Division in Normandy.* Mechanicsburg, PA: Stackpole Books, 1999.

Balkoski, Joseph, *From Beachhead to Brittany: The 29th Infantry Division at Brest, August-September 1944.* Mechanicsburg, PA: Stackpole Books 2008.

Blumenson, Martin, *U.S. Army in World War II,* Chapter XXX The Battle for Brest, www.ibiblio.org/hyperwar/USA/USA-E-Breakout-30.html.

Bradley, Omar, *A General's Life.* New York: Simon and Schuster 1983.

Carafano, James Jay, *After D-Day: Operation Cobra and the Normandy Breakout.* Boulder, Colo: Lynne Rienner Publishers 2000.

Churchill, Winston S., *Triumph and Tragedy.* Boston: Houghton Mifflin Company 1953.

Daugherty, Leo, *The Battle of the Hedgerows: Bradley's First Army in Normandy, June-July 1944.* London: Brown Partworks Limited 2001.

Ellis, John, *Brute Force: Allied Strategy and Tactics in the Second World War.* New York: Viking 1990.

Essame, H., *Patton: A Study in Command.* New York: Charles Scribner's Sons 1974.

Ewing,Joseph H., *29 Let's Go: A History of the 29th Infantry Division in World War II.* Washington, D.C.: Infantry Journal Press, 1948.

Garth, David and Taylor, Charles H., *St-Lo.* Washington D.C.: War Department 1946.

Gawne, Jonathan, *1944, Americans in Brittany: The Battle for Brest.* Paris: Histore & Collections 2002.

Hastings, Max, *Armageddon: The Battle for Germany, 1944-1945.* New York: Alfred A. Knopf 2004.

Hastings, Max, *Overlord: D-Day & the Battle for Normandy.* New York: Simon & Schuster 1984.

Hoyte, Edwin P., *The GI's War: American Soldiers in Europe During World WarII.* New York: De Capo Press 1988.

Johns, Glover S., *The Clay Pigeons of St. Lo.* Mechanicsville, PA: Stackpole Books 2002.

Keegan, John, *Six Armies in Normandy: From D-Day to the Liberation of Paris.* New York: Penguin Books 1982.

Liddell Hart, B.H., *History of the Second World War.* New York: A Perigee Book 1982.

MacDonald, Charles B., *The Mighty Endeavor: The American War in Europe.* New York: Da Capo 1992.

MacDonald, Charles B., *The Siegfried Line Campaign.* Washington, D.C: Center of Military History 1990. www.history.army.mil/books/wwii/Siegfried/Siegfried Line/siegfried.htm

McManus, John C., *The Americans at Normandy: The Summer of 1944--The American War from the Normandy Beaches to Falaise.* New York: Tom Doherty Associates, L.L.C. 2004.

Nisbet, Robert, *Roosevelt and Stalin: The Failed Courtship.* Washington, D.C.: Regnery Gateway, 1988.

Reynolds, Michael, *Eagles and Bulldogs in Normandy 1944.* Havertown, PA: Casemate 2003.

Turner, Barry, *Countdown to Victory: The Final European Campaigns of World War II.* New York: William Morrow 2004.

Weigley, Russell F., *Eisenhower's Lieutenants: The Campaigns of France and Germany, 1944-1945.* 2 Vols. Bloomington, Ind: Indiana University Press 1981.

Whiting, Charles, *West Wall: The Battle for Hitler's Siegfried Line, September 1944-March 1945.* London: Pan Books 2002.

Articles

29 Let's Go, WWII G.I. Stories. Paris: Stars and Stripes 1944-45.
www.lonesentry.com/gi_stories_booklets/29thinfantry
"D-Day to V-E Day," *29 Let's Go*. May 8, 1945
29 Let's Go. February 25, 1945
www.ushmm.org/lc_4/focus/pdf/infantry_29.pdf.

Sempa, Frank F., "First Area Newsman to be Drafted Recalls Horror of Omaha Beach," *Scranton Tribune*, June 1, 1969.

Sempa, Francis P., "William C. Bullitt: Diplomat and Prophet," in the Introduction to William Bullitt, *The Great Globe Itself: A Preface to World Affairs* . New Brunswick, NJ: Transaction Publishers 2005.

Sempa, Francis P., "Somewhere in France, Somewhere in Germany," *American Diplomacy*.http://www.unc.edu/depts/diplomat/item/2008/0406/comm/sempa_somewhere.html.

Sempa, Francis P., "Soldier's Postmark: 'Somewhere in Europe' Letters found in Cellar Tell of Dad's Combat," *Washington Times*.
http://www.washingtontimes.com/news/2008/jun/12/soldiers-postmark-somewhere-in-europe-letters-foun/.

"Ex-Newswriter Battled Way From Normandy Beachhead to Elbe; Gains Discharge on Points," *Scranton Tribune*. July 9, 1945.

Index

About the Author

Francis P. Sempa is the author of *Geopolitics: From the Cold War to the 21st Century* and *America's Global Role: Essays and Reviews on National Security, Geopolitics and War*. He has authored lengthy introductions to four books on U.S. foreign policy, and has written on historical and foreign policy topics for *Strategic Review, American Diplomacy, Presidential Studies Quarterly, The National Interest, National Review, Human Rights Review, International Social Science Review*, the *Washington Times*, and the *Thomas M. Cooley Law Review*. He is a contributor to *The Conduct of American Foreign Policy Debated*. He is an Assistant U.S. Attorney for the Middle District of Pennsylvania, an adjunct professor of political science at Wilkes University, and a contributing editor of *American Diplomacy*.